Board Games

Board Games

STRAIGHT TALK FOR NEW DIRECTORS AND GOOD GOVERNANCE

John T. Montford and
Joseph Daniel McCool

Foreword by Herb Kelleher

⬤ PRAEGER™

An Imprint of ABC-CLIO, LLC
Santa Barbara, California • Denver, Colorado

Library of Congress Cataloging-in-Publication Data

Names: Montford, John T., 1943- author. | McCool, Joseph Daniel, author.
Title: Board games : straight talk for new directors and good governance /
    John T. Montford and Joseph Daniel McCool ; foreword by Herb Kelleher.
Description: Santa Barbara : Praeger, 2016. | Includes bibliographical
    references and index.
Identifiers: LCCN 2016003439 | ISBN 9781440842528 (hardback) |
    ISBN 9781440842535 (ebook)
Subjects: LCSH: Boards of directors. | Corporate governance. | Management.
Classification: LCC HD2745 .M68 2016 | DDC 658.4/22—dc23
LC record available at https://lccn.loc.gov/2016003439

ISBN: 978-1-4408-4252-8
EISBN: 978-1-4408-4253-5

20   19   18   17   16   4   5

This book is also available as an eBook.

Praeger
An Imprint of ABC-CLIO, LLC

ABC-CLIO, LLC
130 Cremona Drive, P.O. Box 1911
Santa Barbara, California 93116-1911
www.abc-clio.com

This book is printed on acid-free paper ∞

Manufactured in the United States of America

This book and any related digital or electronic forms are intended for educational and informational purposes only. The authors have made every reasonable effort to present accurate and up-to-date information in this book. However, neither the authors nor the publisher is engaged in rendering legal or accounting advice, and nothing in this book is intended to be or should be construed as such. If the reader deems such professional advice necessary or desirable, the reader is advised to consult with his or her own attorney, accountant, and/or other advisor regarding the specific situation in question. In addition, neither the authors nor the publisher assumes any responsibility for any errors or omissions. The authors and the publisher specifically disclaim any liability resulting from the use or application of the information contained in this book. This book contains references to federal law. In addition to federal law, the reader is advised that state laws would also apply in connection with his or her role as a director. This book is not intended to provide information on state laws, which vary by jurisdiction.

For Ford, Maylin, Anistin, and John Dylan

and

For Lindsay, Erin, Matthew, and Sean

Contents

Foreword

I have known John Montford for many decades, as a friend, member of the USMC, eminently successful lawyer, powerful political leader, important business leader, higher education leader, creative participant in numerous charitable endeavors, and superb member of the Board of Directors of Southwest Airlines. His variegated experience, tough-minded pragmatism, keen powers of analysis and concise explications, and his West Texas common sense are a unique adornment to any organization he joins. By virtue of this collaboration with John, I know Joseph McCool must be a thoughtful and effective leader as well.

Board Games is a compendium of knowledge and advice, traversing the entire spectrum of how you get "invited to the party" through how you should behave "at the bar" once you are there. With respect to its coverage of board directorships, of any kind, it is the equivalent of the *Oxford English Dictionary*'s status with respect to coverage of the English language.

You don't have to agree with every single asseveration and with every atmospheric and tonality within the covers of *Board Games* to profit from its superabundance of nuggets. But if you have any interest, personal or purely intellectual, in the subject of directorships, *Board Games* is your "mother lode" for thinking about boards and how they should be constituted, function, and perform.

Board memberships are no longer merely a "safe harbor" for college fraternity brothers. Boards are under ever increasing media, regulatory, and shareholder scrutiny, and their work is essential to the continued efflorescence of the free enterprise, market economy in America; e.g., no, don't invest our company's cash in subprime mortgages!

John and Joseph, in *Board Games*, have produced a fundamental and provocative text that clearly shows that "old-fashioned" boards have gone the way of buckboard carriages, and I thank them for their seminal work.

—Herb Kelleher, co-founder, Chairman Emeritus, and former CEO, Southwest Airlines

Acknowledgments

A special thanks to my wife and confidante, Debbie Montford, for her keen insights on nonprofit boards; to my longtime executive assistant, Cappy Robnett, for all the countless hours of transcribing my draft pages; to John Keeton of Covenant Multi Family Organization, my financial advisers, for helping with corporate finance and balance sheets; to Herb Kelleher and Colleen Barrett for imparting a lifetime of good management techniques; to Vickie Shuler for finding Herb when we needed him; to Tom Pitcher for help on the Fleetwood story; to all my fellow directors on both corporate and nonprofits who have graduated from the school of "hard knocks"; and to Gaylord Armstrong for proofreading.

Other special thanks go to Mike Wheless, who introduced the co-authors based on his conviction that our unique insights and experience could help directors change the game of corporate governance. And also to the Honorable Dale W. Meyerrose, Major General, U.S. Air Force (Retired), one of the world's leading experts on the cyber industry, whose views on data strategy, security, and more added real depth to this endeavor. And we would be remiss if we didn't also offer our profound thanks to Hilary Claggett, Senior Editor, Business, Economics & Finance at Praeger Publishing/ABC-CLIO, whose work and support also made this book possible.

We are further indebted to the late Dr. Tory Herring, the CEO of Leadership Partners. Tory's example, partnership, and friendship, and later his untimely passing as we were finishing the manuscript for this book, deepened our resolve to reflect his lessons in humility, coaching, organization development, and what it means to lead "a life well lived" in these pages.

From his days playing football on scholarship at Georgia Tech, through his distinguished service flying helicopters in Vietnam with the unit featured in the movie *Apocalypse Now*, to earning two doctoral degrees in individual and group behavior and dynamics, racing with the Porsche club, and committing to his family, Tory set an amazing leadership example for us all. Combined, his life and professional work experience provided a realistic perspective on leadership and organization development and the capacity for relating to people at all levels of today's organizations with credibility, humility, and sincerity. In closing, as Dr. Herring reflected on his life, he said "I have had many people give me a second chance and contribute to my success and want to do the same for others."

Introduction

Throughout my many jobs—from the United States Marine Corps to election as a district attorney in Texas and later to the Texas Senate, later to appointment as chancellor of Texas Tech University System, as an executive at AT&T and consultant for General Motors, and now as an independent corporate director and public policy consultant—I have had the privilege of serving on just about every kind of board imaginable.

These include the boards of charitable organizations, nonprofits, publicly owned and private companies, as well as *Fortune* 500 companies like Southwest Airlines. To this day, I continue to serve as president of a private foundation board.

As you invest valuable time with this book, I suggest that after long years of boardroom service and learning, one thing is certain:

If you are selected for service on a formal board of directors or a more informal advisory board, whether public or private, nonprofit or for-profit, be it a large, perhaps global institution or a small company, you will experience an important part of the "American dream."

Service on a board presents powerful opportunities to extend or advance one's career, to stay connected to an industry and professional peers, and to lend a unique voice to the most critical governance issues and challenges of our times. It is also much more.

Your commitment to effective boardroom stewardship is a vital, but often unrecognized part of the fabric of American business and the U.S. economy, and increasingly, a model for the most important work of every organization around the world.

It's been said that the best and worst things that happen to any organization have their genesis in the boardroom. The decisions and oversight of those charged with protecting the interests of shareholders, employees, customers, and other constituents whose lives and/or livelihoods may be on the line are absolutely critical to the sustainability of the organization, its mission, and its actual work. That is an important perspective for any new or established director to bring to every key decision.

We have done business this way in this country for a long, long time. There is simply no getting around the fact that board service is an important component that helps make free enterprise work. It is true even if you are on a charitable or nonprofit board because you're likely going to help fill a void of public service that government cannot or should not.

I can think of many instances, particularly when the U.S. economy has faltered, when charitable boards have played a critical role in helping support the less fortunate members of society who might otherwise have "fallen through the cracks" of government-administered programs and who also lack the hand of opportunity that many of us have seen extended throughout our careers.

Although the focus of this book is largely on for-profit board service, never discount the importance of all types of boardroom service including charitable and nonprofits because such service is an important part of the fabric of American society and the U.S. economy.

Congratulations to you if you have been selected to serve as a member of a board of directors. Chances are you were selected because you were well connected, successful in your own right, and display a level of competence and talent that your advocates felt would add value to an enterprise.

For-profit board service is, in part, a fulfillment of the American dream—you are now a part of a business that exists to make a profit and create value for your shareholders.

And that brings us to another point—making a profit is not un-American, and it is not a concept you ever need to apologize for as long as you are doing it legally and ethically.

The profit motive has long differentiated our U.S. economy from many other economies around the world, particularly those where dictators or despots or warlords rule, or where it is thought government can do it better—which is a formula for disaster in most cases.

In the United States, we are blessed to exist in a free enterprise system where we can, through our own ingenuity and entrepreneurial drive, make some money and in the case of your board service, make money for your shareholders.

If you are new to the boardroom, I wish you well and hope this book proves a trusted guide on what will undoubtedly prove a journey full of lessons about the organization and effective governance of boards, the critical nature of CEO and board director succession, and the unshakeable merit of common sense.

If you are a veteran of boardroom politics and the human elements that shape them, I trust you may empathize with some of the lessons from my own journey in important board director seats and find a few gems or simple reminders about why people like us make such a commitment to the organizations we serve.

Throughout the pages of this book, you will gain not only from my experience and perspective, but that of my friend and co-author, Joseph Daniel McCool. For nearly 20 years, Joe has been a globally recognized expert on executive search, board director recruitment, and corporate talent strategy, advising some of North America's largest and most successful companies on how to align talent and leadership with profits and performance. He brings exceptional insight into making the board nominating process far more effective, more inclusive, and more sustainable. In my view, there is no better qualified adviser to today's board nominating committees than my esteemed co-author. You will assuredly gain from Joe's valuable insights, as have I, co-authoring this book.

You will note as you read on, by the way, that I have taken some poetic license, occasionally retelling my personal experiences in the first person, while on other pages leaning more to second- and third-person references to more effectively convey our message. Joe and I both felt it was important to infuse some of my personal experiences to illustrate the real-life situations that have helped inform the pages and perspectives that follow, yet also to demonstrate our alignment on most of the key strategic issues addressed here.

Thank you for investing your time in our book. And remember, your contribution as a member of a formal board or advisory board helps grease the wheels of our global economy one lesson, one relationship, and one board meeting at a time.

Respectfully,
John T. Montford
San Antonio, Texas

Chapter 1

How to Get Appointed to a Board When You're Not a Household Name: Bring Something the Board Wants but Doesn't Have

"How can I get appointed to a board?" It is a question we are asked frequently by up-and-coming, high-performing professional men and women and just as often by established, long-tenured leaders and chief executives who view an appointment to a corporate board of directors as the pinnacle, defining achievement of their careers.

Getting the call to the boardroom is a testament to a successful career. It is a special recognition of hard work, experience, and expertise, and one typically reserved for individuals who have conducted themselves as consummate professionals while building their credentials—and, just as important, their peer relationships and professional networks.

Being asked to serve on a corporate or not-for-profit board or even an organization's advisory board is clearly an invitation to participate in the American dream. It represents an open door and a world of possibilities and learning. It demands an increasing amount of due diligence to determine which board is right for you and whether you're up to the expectations of a board that asks you to join.

Straight Talk: Know what you are signing up for.

A call to the boardroom should be received as both a special opportunity and a personal calling—a calling to service and to stewardship of institutional and shareholder concerns. It now demands a willingness to learn what it takes to be an effective director in an age of continued glo-balization, activism, and growing calls for the kind of servant leadership that puts others first.

It would be easy, given some human tendencies, to use a board ap-pointment as a reason to gloat, to inflate an already healthy ego, and to trumpet the latest in your string of achievements. If you are so inclined, you'd better find some other place to channel your energy.

What is interesting—and telling about your success as a director sitting in a paid, corporate board seat or in a volunteer role with a not-for-profit, charitable, or advisory board—is that everything that brought you to this pinnacle moment is now set aside so you can focus on the company and work with other directors and management.

Part of the allure of a boardroom appointment is the public acknowl-edgment of your business savvy, experience, and expertise—and, perhaps most of all, its exclusive nature. Many are qualified, yet few are asked to serve, for reasons we will explain later in this chapter.

But the real key to your success in the boardroom will be to remind yourself, at the start of every single board meeting, that the call to the boardroom is a call to serve. It is an invitation to work hard, do your homework, show up, and contribute to the board's business in a way that leverages what you know and need to know, as well as your willing-ness to put in the time to do the job well.

So revel in getting the call. Celebrate with family and friends. Feel good about yourself, then set to work immediately putting others' inter-ests at the fore.

PRACTICAL OBSERVATIONS ABOUT THE BOARDROOM

While many highly accomplished men and women hope and expect to get that call to the boardroom some day, the truth is that few are asked to serve organizations in such a critical governance role.

Unless you have the wide name recognition of a former secretary of state, cabinet secretary, or U.S. senator, or you have celebrity status as a high-profile chief executive officer, you're not going to be openly solicited for board service. Individuals like Condoleezza Rice and Bill Gates are going to get calls about serving on boards. People with incredibly high name recognition will get those calls. And when you consider that shares of Weight Watchers soared in October 2015 upon the news that Oprah Winfrey would be joining its board of directors and taking a 10 percent stake with options to acquire another 5 percent stake, you can expect the big names to get even more of those calls.[1]

However, for most people without household name appeal, the pathway is clear—we have to earn it. There simply is no big "easy" button to push for appointment to the boardroom. It is for this reason we committed to put together this roadmap for getting to the board appointment you want and which you may also deserve.

Many accomplished executives would like to serve on a board of directors. Appointment to a major corporate board may bring significant compensation. Appointments to the board of a smaller, private company or the governing or advisory board of a start-up company, a not-for-profit, charitable, philanthropic, and/or community or institutional board all stoke executive-level interest.

Yet if we consider the actual number of annual appointments to paid corporate board positions each year, we see that only a small fraction of those who would like to serve in such a stewardship role will receive the call.

So what separates those who actually get appointed from all those who would simply like to get appointed?

These factors are particularly important qualifiers for securing a board appointment:

1. Your reputation, experience, and credentials for a board appointment
2. The expert knowledge and insight you bring and how it will extend and deepen board competency in the right areas, at the right time
3. The networking relationships and advocates you can engage to rise above other successful leaders
4. The clarity, consistency, and conviction of your own efforts to engage with influential people

So how do *you* get on a board?

The answer is, a lifetime of hard work creates what, more now than ever before, represents only an opportunity to do more hard work in today's corporate boardroom under an intensifying glare of public opinion, shareholder advocates, activists, lawyers, labor unions, the media, and more.

But to get there, you have to have a plan and stick with it. Of course, luck also factors into the board appointment equation. Be at the right place, at the right time, with the right people. You can control two of those variables. As for timing, well, let us just say we hope luck is on your side.

If you bring more than one of the above-listed attributes to a board, there is still no guarantee that you will get the board appointment you desire. You still have to make it happen.

As a practical matter, you have to set your sights on getting a board appointment and go after it if you want it. Interest in serving is not enough to get to the boardroom. That is true for paid corporate board directorships, although your willingness to volunteer may indeed qualify you for any number of not-for-profit, charitable, or community boards or advisory boards.

When it comes to securing a paid corporate board seat, do not expect your own fairy board-mother to flitter her wings heralding a major board appointment while you sip a martini on your back porch. That is, unless you are cavorting with some of the best-known names in business, government, civic affairs, or perhaps the worlds of media or sports. Those relationships may help you to get where you want to go.

But the right path is the path that will work.

> **Our Straight Talk on how to get appointed to a board is simple: you are going to have to earn it. You are going to have to work for it if this is what you really want. You are going to have to set your sights on it and go after it.**

The truth is, you are going to have to plan for it—and put that plan into action over time.

Yet before you can build your own plan, let us consider what boards are looking for, the different paths that would position you as a highly qualified potential candidate for a board seat, and some other timeless lessons on getting to the boardroom and making a difference once you get there.

> **Straight Talk: Know what boards are looking for.**

It is hard to serve a need until you understand that need.

In order to get to the boardroom, you must understand what boards want, what they need, and what is motivating their directors to seek new competencies that will improve governance and, in some cases, cover their rear ends if something goes wrong. (Be sure to read chapter 4, "When Bad Things Happen to Good Boards.")

As has been the case for decades, today's boards of directors do not want to be taken by surprise or be caught unaware. The last thing anyone wants is to see his or her name associated with damaging headlines splashed one morning all over the front page of the *Wall Street Journal* or the *Financial Times*.

Contemporary board directors want to be regularly briefed on emerging threats to and opportunities for the business. They want to engage with board peers they like and respect. They want to safeguard shareholder interests, contribute meaningfully to corporate strategy, plan for the eventual succession of the chief executive (if they are doing their jobs), and ensure the growth of total returns to shareholders over time.

To achieve these goals, they need smart people assembled around the boardroom table who are open-minded and dedicated to put in the hours it now requires to be a good board director.

> **Straight Talk: To get yourself appointed to the boardroom these days, you have to bring both the "who" and the "what" factors directors believe they need to add to their boards.**

THE "WHO" BOARDS NEED

Today's boards are looking for globally experienced business executives. They are looking for big thinkers who can implement ideas. They want successful women and other accomplished professionals who would add racial, cultural, and ethnic diversity to their boards, in part to reflect greater connectivity to globalizing consumer groups.

Progressive boards now seek successful individuals from all fields—from business to law and politics and from academia, science, and public service. They want innovators and boundary spanners. They want people who are wise enough to think for themselves and bold enough to stand up for what they believe.

Just as every diamond is a lump of coal that "did well under pressure," a good board director brings well-developed soft skills, hard skills, people skills, and exemplary behaviors and actions born in the crucible of organizational challenge and healthy conflict. Among the attributes boards seek and find highly desirable, executive coach Kevin Arvin adds, is *leadership courage*—characterized by a balance between high candor and high respect.

Individuals who feel an obligation to bring a different perspective to the board, who understand that it is not how well you "sing in unison" with the board, but how often you add a unique voice, can serve a critical role in advancing the board's effectiveness.

Boards want people willing to stand firm, if necessary, when it comes to principle. Yet they also want men and women who understand that negotiation, compromise, and straight talk and candor might land them in the minority of directors on a certain issue, but that it is important to engage gracefully and unify quickly for the sake of the bigger picture.

Also in high demand are individuals who have demonstrated sound business judgment and who bring a solid reputation. Boards want men and women of integrity and character. They want people who are dignified and true. They want directors with a confident, inquiring, but likeable demeanor.

They require leaders who are honest, straightforward, highly informed, and deeply engaged. They need individuals who want to serve for the right reasons—a purpose that transcends their own needs and rather, puts the focus on what is truly good and sustainable for the enterprise, no matter the industry, region, or brand.

Whether a paid role or not, a board appointment demands the "volunteer" mindset—the passionate commitment and selfless devotion of a person who serves for all the right reasons, says executive coach Kevin Arvin. The service-oriented leader is motivated to bring about the best outcomes for an organization to which he or she, in many cases, had no previous obligation or connection—a true servant leader.

If it sounds as if we are describing someone who is almost too good to be true, that is correct.

Boards want—and need—men and women of uncommon ability and experience for a uniquely individual challenge. Yes, discerning directors want the moon and the stars when it comes to picking one of their own. After all, they understand the power and influence that will be bestowed on the next director and want to work with a peer of the highest order.

That is why the boardroom is rarified air. Some of the most important things that happen to companies and to leaders at every level of the organization have their genesis in the boardroom.

The search for the best board directors is, in part, a search for the true potential of the organization and what it can deliver to its shareholders, be they stockholders, employees and their families, vendors and suppliers, and, of course, customers and business partners.

It is only natural that the boardroom be reserved for men and women of distinction who by their words and deeds qualify uniquely to serve the best interests of these greater and far wider constituents.

THE "WHAT" BOARDS NEED

If you have the right stuff to check a board's "Who" sniff test, as we have outlined above, it is time to take a serious look at the "What" you would bring to the table.

The "What" is the board's answer to all the new pressures it may be facing, particularly corporate boards, which are facing almost dizzying pressures on an ever widening range of topics from an increasingly diverse and disparate group of activist shareholders, media, employees, regulators, and more.

Is your chief executive officer really worth all that he or she is being paid? What do you make of the latest cybersecurity breach at your competitor and what are you doing about it? Is this corporate strategy the right one to beat low-cost market disrupters? Why isn't the company committed to higher dividends? Why aren't there more women and minorities in the executive leadership of the enterprise? And shouldn't the roles of chair and CEO be split?

These are just some of the new and emerging questions that are keeping board directors awake at night. That is, aside from all the reading material they must now pore over in advance of every single meeting of the board if they are to avoid being blindsided, jailed (for financial impropriety on their watch), or looking unprepared.

It is for these reasons that boards are spending more time than ever before on assessing their own strengths and weaknesses via a board evaluation. Serious boards are taking stock of their composition and what they know. Just as important, they are identifying serious gaps in knowledge, skills, and structure and how filling those gaps can be addressed via the addition of a new crop of board directors.

To say there is more scrutiny on board director nomination and succession today would be an understatement. There is more pressure to get director selection decisions right, and the best path to that end is to understand what the board lacks, what it needs, and how it can be improved.

Today, boards of every variety (corporate, charitable, advisory, academic, and community) want people who bring that certain "What" factor that is something unique to offer in terms of adding to the board's overall competency and functionality—a particular area of expertise like antitrust, cybersecurity, executive search or human resources, and tax and compliance, to name just a few.

Straight Talk: You have to have something unique and relevant to offer to qualify for a board of directors and get the board interested in you.

There are actually a lot of "What" variables—individual competencies that any board might really value. They are as unique as the individuals who bring these experiences and competencies.

The power of "What" really gets to the question of "What has he done?" or "What has she done?" The answers to these questions point directly to the kind of straight talk guidance about how to attain that special something that boards will find attractive in you.

Experience tells us there are actually several pathways to secure a board appointment. The real difference, as executive recruiter Mike Wheless of retained executive search firm Wheless Partners has shared with us time and again, is to have what boards want and get them to take notice.

The following pathways and actionable goals to qualify for the boardroom might just give you the "What" you need to stand out from the crowd of others who would themselves like to serve as a board director:

Be a success story. Successful people from all walks of life have what it takes not only to be appointed to a board but also to serve as exceptionally effective directors. To be a success, you must be successful at making a commitment to something you really believe in and giving it all you have to make it work.

Some of the best known and highest performing companies on earth learned long ago that enabling successful people to recruit other successful people into the organization creates its own multiplier effect. Successful people want to be surrounded by other people who are successful. Although it is important to note that poor leadership or a culture of overwork can ruin it all.

Positive energy, teamwork among highly accomplished peers, and a sense that the enterprise is attracting the best and brightest builds to the point where team success is inevitable.

If you can create your own success story, it will provide a powerful narrative backdrop against which to frame your unique qualifications to serve as a board director. In fact, you will learn that as soon as others witness your success, they will gravitate toward you. You will be asked to serve on a variety of community and charitable boards, and cheerful service to those groups will set you up quite nicely to be recognized as a potential candidate for a seat on a corporate board, perhaps that of a publicly traded company.

Start your own company. Become a successful entrepreneur. Successful business owners usually garner a lot of attention. This is often reflected in local and regional media and in the communities where they are based and where they employ people.

Starting your own business takes courage and guts. It requires vision and boldness. It demands focus and discipline and flexibility in ways that other life opportunities do not. It can be all-consuming, so be careful. But most of all, be confident and be yourself.

As you plant the seeds of your own business and become a successful entrepreneur, do so knowing that you will be building a very attractive building block for service on a board of directors. If you've already built a successful business, you may already know the key lessons that another company would welcome as new insight to go farther, go faster, and go beyond.

Successful entrepreneurs often make fantastic board directors—that is, if they have their head screwed on correctly. An entrepreneur who can learn to be a collaborator and a team player can bring real-world experience and expertise to boards that really need it.

Be an investor. Hitch your wagon to a promising start-up company. Get in on the ground floor. Put your money behind your enthusiasm about a new company's innovative product or service. Attend and participate in shareholder meetings.

If you can help conceptualize a company, commercialize its idea(s), and put your money where your mouth is, your standing as an investor will indeed move others to take notice and provide a platform to leverage your financial influence. Enough said.

Increase the diversity of a board. Women leaders and leaders from underrepresented racial, cultural, and ethnic minority groups—particularly those with a track record of success in business enterprise—have not received enough consideration for paid, public company board seats. That is in large part because today's boards are still largely comprised of directors who found their way to the boardroom via the good ol' boys club.

Things are beginning to change, but not nearly fast enough because the board nominating process remains handicapped by insular thinking. There remains significant ignorance about how to really diversify management and the board and why boards' chosen search firms haven't been getting it done. Boards simply are not pushing themselves, their Nominating Committees, and corporate heads of Human Resources with the right questions, the right recruiting partners, and fresh perspectives.

After all, you will have a hard time convincing these co-authors that only former corporate chief executive officers are fit for board service. That view has helped exclude many great candidates from too many corporate boards, and that needs to change. Now.

Many of today's directors were appointed almost exclusively based on whom they knew at the time (it helped if a chummy CEO was already serving on your board), where they went to school, and/or because they were in the right place at the right time and looked and sounded like the rest of the board. Things are changing for the better. Women and minority board candidates are getting more of the consideration they deserve, but there is also a caution here for them.

If you are a woman or bring a diversity profile and you do get called to serve in the boardroom, make sure that you have more to add to the board's discussion than your own personal advocacy for getting more people on the board like you. You have to build credibility with your peers on a variety of issues, not just the challenge of making boardrooms more diverse. It is vital that you not forget the big picture. Educate your board peers about where you stand, remind them if necessary, but do not turn any one issue (even the important business of diversifying the boardroom) into your own personal soapbox lest you run the social risk of being marginalized for it. Earn the trust of your peers. Push for reform. Understand the personal dynamics, and forge ahead on the course of reform with the trust and group support you need.

Serve with distinction, first and foremost. Let others notice your exceptional contributions to the board above all else, and maybe then your board peers will realize that not every director hails from the same background and that there is real value in a diversity of experience, perspective, and life history on the board.

Intellectual diversity alone, as we were reminded by the esteemed Tory Herring, PsyD, PhD, and chief executive of Leadership Partners, a leading organizational and leadership development advisory firm with offices around the world, is key for boards of directors to function at their highest potential. You will gain from many of Tory's insights in chapter 11, and we regret that his recent passing will leave some part of his important work unfinished.

Demonstrate you know more about the company's industry, markets, customers, competitors, and supply chain. If you can convince a board of directors that it's missing the boat, pursuing a flawed strategy, or otherwise missing a big opportunity, you might just garner the attention you would need to convince its members that you would be right for their board.

Fill an important gap in the current board's vision of vital market, competitor, regulatory, and/or consumer indicators, and you will immediately differentiate yourself from all the other would-be board directors who might try to engage on their respective "Who" qualifications alone.

Volunteer for a charitable organization's board of directors. Volunteer your time, talent, and treasure to a charitable board or some other mission-driven entity to gain valuable experience and to increase and diversify your professional network relationships. Many not-for-profit boards could gain considerably from your service and perspective and offer you the fulfillment that comes from helping others and giving back.

Many of these boards are comprised of highly successful, widely interconnected individuals from a variety of backgrounds. You might be surprised by just how well connected they are. Rest assured, they will take notice of anyone who shows real commitment to the kinds of "hands-on" work these appointments require. Your success as a key contributor to the health of these organizations can really get you noticed.

A lot of times serving on a nonprofit, doing a good job, and serving alongside some heavyweights means they will notice you and may recommend you for serving on a corporate board that pays you. So do not discount the potential influence and professional networking connectivity of nonprofit boards and advisory committees. You will meet a lot of people, including a lot of very powerful and influential people, and that is a great help in getting on your first corporate board.

If you can be successful at this level, it is an exceptional audition for service to even the biggest of multibillion-dollar global corporate boards. Often, you will find that outstanding service to one not-for-profit board begets appointments to other boards. Just be careful not to overcommit.

Build a reputation as an effective fundraiser. This can go hand-in-hand with service to a charitable organization's board. If you're gifted at demonstrating a compelling need and making "the big ask," even in political or academic circles, you will win the support of a wide variety of people. After all, without a budget and your work as a fundraiser, the organization or campaign you care so deeply about and have chosen to serve likely would not be able to fulfill its mission. Of course, you'll be a far more credible fundraiser if you yourself have been as generous as you can be.

DEVELOPING YOUR OWN BOARD APPOINTMENT ACTION PLAN

You may be setting yourself up nicely for just such an appointment if you can bring significant "Who" and "What" qualifications to a board of directors.

But experience proves and straight talk demands we share that it is simply not going to happen without a consistent, multipoint effort to make others aware of those qualifications and your interest in applying all you would bring to a board.

The truth is you are not going to get a board appointment unless sitting board directors believe you have earned it and unless they are convinced you are going to make them look good by bringing something of real value to their team. They cannot reach those conclusions without some help.

That is why it is so important not only to have the credibility for a board role, but also a concerted action plan that inserts you and your reputation in just the right conversations. You have to be positioned effectively as an exceptional "get" for the board. You have to convey— or have others do it for you—some level of interest in at least exploring the possibility of joining the board. And you have to be prepared to present yourself—and your experience—in the best possible ways. The following tactics will help you get there:

Networking. It should almost go without saying that no matter how well known you are and how much your accomplishments are appreciated by others, it pays to continue expanding your professional and personal networks. A range of business networking websites makes that easier today than ever before.

It is up to you to market yourself or have others very selectively do it for you.

Caution: There is a very fine line between making your interest in a board appointment known to others and being perceived as selling or promoting yourself in a way that will be a turnoff to the very people you would try to influence. This is particularly true for "network" connections you don't know well or whom you've never met personally. Remember, at the most senior levels, board directors want to choose you. You will not sell directly to them.

Let your closest peers and friends know that you would be willing to consider a board appointment. Tell them why and what you would add to a board. If they see it and understand it, with your approval they will let others know and before you know it the word-of-mouth may just lead to your getting the call you have been waiting for.

Engage an executive search or board search firm. If you have truly been successful in business or some other walk of life, it is likely you have already built relationships with executive search firms that occasionally recruit for their clients' boards.

If you have not, do some research and figure out who knows executive search firms and can make a personal introduction of you (Hint: This advice is often followed by the words, "Get McCool or Montford on the phone."), since most retained executive search firms will not acknowledge you if you come knocking on your own. This is truly one of those

"Don't call us, we'll call you" situations that reflects the power of who you know or who you can get to and whose support you can enlist.

If you have been named to a corporate board or a high-profile not-for-profit, you will find it is easier to get named to another board because you are seen as a known commodity. Once a search firm views you as a marketable asset, it will market your experience—and your board experience—as never before because you are perceived as a safe bet.

Caution: Some search firms may be shopping multiple high-profile candidates to multiple client boards at any one time. Unless you know you are in the pole position or are willing to boldly engage with a prospective board peer while being careful not to oversell, it could be a waste of your time.

Leverage or develop relationships with high-power people who can lobby for you. Who do you know who might make an introduction for you? Who could give you a great recommendation as a business partner, a colleague, a consultant, or a savvy business expert? One of the best ways to curry favor with board directors is to get to know them, get to know what makes them tick, and find areas of common interest with them.

If you can engage personally with sitting board members, that is great. If you cannot at present, map out who knows them and how you might get introduced and acquainted.

Build a boardroom portfolio. One of the best ways to lobby for your own appointment to a board is to build a portfolio of background information that can quickly get others up to speed on your experience, education, accomplishments, and what you have to offer.

Build a convincing and compelling boardroom portfolio of your experience, qualifications, and expertise that explains why you would make an outstanding board director. Develop a plan and let your boardroom portfolio outline reasons for others to market you as a great director candidate. If you don't make others aware of your interest in a board appointment, no one will do that for you. You have to go after it if you really want it. A boardroom portfolio can speak volumes for you and can be conveniently passed around by members of a board.

Straight Talk: Do your homework, and realize not every board is right for you.

It is very important to understand that not every board may be right for you.

Before accepting an invitation to join any board, it is imperative to check out the organization's track record and research its history, governance and legal structure, its financial performance, customer base, corporate strategy, mission and purpose, and expectations of directors.

Particularly in industries that are heavily regulated such as financial services, a failure to conduct serious due diligence on a prospective company and its board could, at a later date, spiral into a real personal disaster for your career and your reputation, too.

Before you accept any board appointment, it is critical that you do your homework and understand the board's expectations of individual directors. That includes examining its directors and officers (D&O) liability insurance policy and getting your own lawyer's insight on what it may mean for you. There are risks associated with paid service to a corporate board, in particular, so it's vital to engage legal due diligence to make sure you're not leaving yourself exposed to litigation.

You must review a board's written bylaws and anything it stipulates in writing regarding expectations of board members, including issues related to tenure, reappointment, and dismissal terms. It makes sense to inquire about anticipated time commitment and scheduled board meetings. If you can't show up, you can't contribute as an effective director.

If you are joining a not-for-profit or charitable board, now would be the time to inquire about the expected financial support from board members. It is likely that one of these boards may already have a sense of your potential level of giving, but it would be wise to discuss these expectations before you accept an appointment.

You should ask to speak with, or better yet, to meet with current board members to get their sense of the organization's strategy, and to understand some of the interpersonal dynamics that shape the board's working agenda, relationships, and communications.

Be mindful: A lot of what's important to know about any board you might consider joining won't be found on paper. You'll have to find out the unwritten rules of how the board operates and the social dynamics that make it work—or which create tension you may not want to become part of.

It is important to check out an enterprise's track record and its financial statements. You should know something about its current chief executive or executive director, in the case of not-for-profits, and that person's reputation. Get to know the organization's mission, brand identity, and how well it is fulfilling its promise.

As with so many things in life, it is really buyer beware as you evaluate whether to join a board.

> **Straight Talk: Financial institutions are a special challenge. There is heavy regulation in the banking world. If you don't invest serious due diligence before you join the board of a financial services institution, your decision could end in personal disaster.**

One person known to one of this book's co-authors served on multiple boards and had to jump through a lot of hoops just to qualify for continued service to one of the financial services company boards on which he served.

Financial institutions merit careful scrutiny when it comes to going on their boards. There are just a lot of potential hassles and intrusions into your life that could result because these companies are so heavily regulated. The hassle involved simply may not be worth it to you, let alone the time commitment required to serve effectively as a steward of these companies' shareholders.

When it comes to financial institutions, be careful. An appointment to a board in that industry may get you a whole lot more than you bargained for.

Of all the directors this same co-author has known, bank directors complain more than anyone about all the details they have to attend to and hoops they have to jump through. Be careful what you ask for because you may not find the right fit on a bank's board of directors.

The straight talk is that financial services appointments may require the most stringent forms of due diligence on any new board director appointee. Unless you're really willing to be examined five ways to Sunday, it may not be worth the hassle.

> **Straight Talk: *Always* return your calls.**

Over the course of our respective careers, we have seen more than a handful of corporate initiatives, focus group–driven ideas, and even executive job offers go by the wayside due only to the lack of a returned phone call or a related disconnect. This again underscores our earlier note on being in the right place at the right time.

You should simply make it a habit to return phone calls. We can testify to that from experience because one of your co-authors—we'll simply refer to him here by his nickname of "Montford"—was almost a casualty of a failure to return an important phone call from one of the most successful names in corporate America.

In the spring of 2002, Ed Whitacre, the iconic CEO of AT&T and General Motors, had just named John president of external affairs for Southwestern Bell Corporation. This was one of many exciting roles Montford has had the privilege of serving in throughout several different chapters of a long career.

John remembers running into Herb Kelleher, the legendary chair and CEO of Southwest Airlines who graciously authored the foreword to this book, in 2002 at a black-tie affair to which we had both been invited. Herb was fully himself, sipping Wild Turkey from a carafe captioned "Kelleher Special Reserve" and smoking cigarettes like a wood-burning stove. "Hey Senator—Chancellor," he quipped, "You never returned my call from last year, so I shelved what I was calling you about. Oh yes, it was to see if you would be interested in going on the board of Southwest Airlines!"

John remembers he gasped for air. Montford had always made it a point to return phone calls and would never have neglected a call from anyone, especially Herb Kelleher. John said, "Herb, it is all my fault."

John was chancellor of Texas Tech University and resigned in July 2001 to join SBC and Southwestern Bell. He had changed jobs and changed cell phone numbers and simply did not get the call from Herb. Stupid me, he thought. He always prided himself on returning calls, but something evidently went really wrong when he switched phones and telephone numbers in transitioning to a new job.

At that black-tie exchange with Herb, John did not know what to say to him other than to admit his guilt and to explain how he changed phones and added a new cell phone number when he left Texas Tech to join SBC. Turns out Herb's first call and voice message was left on a Texas Tech answering machine that was left sitting in a box in a university IT department closet.

"Gosh, Herb, I hope you will forgive my neglect in not forwarding my calls from my old number. Here is my new cell number. I would love to join your board," John remembers telling him.

"Well, to tell you the truth," Herb replied, "with the ensuing tragedy of 9/11 and all the calamity it caused in this country and in particular the airline industry, we have not proceeded to fill that vacancy. So, I will talk to the board and let you know."

After several weeks, John was about to chalk this one up to his own bad judgment and a costly lack of follow-up on his part when he received a letter from Herb asking him to join the Southwest Airlines board of directors. John called him at once and said it would be an honor for him to serve on the board. Now, about a dozen years later, John is still there on the Southwest Airlines board of directors. He also serves in the important role of chair of its Audit Committee.

So what is the lesson here for today's board directors and prospective board candidates? Always, always, always return your calls! Unfortunately, for those who do not figure things out in time, the call that comes (and subsequently goes unnoticed) is often interpreted in these terms: "I thought you didn't return the call because you weren't interested."

What an incredible opportunity and an instructive lesson—always return your calls and if you change jobs or phone numbers, forward your old number for calls to your new one. It is also wise to make sure everyone in your contact database knows your new email address, too. Especially today, you always have to be reachable by telephone, mobile phone, email, social media, videoconference applications, and whatever means possible when critical business decisions and board succession opportunities come knocking.

So why did Herb Kelleher ask John to serve on the Southwest board?

Montford had been a successful district attorney and an influential member of the Texas Senate. Additionally, he had been a very successful chancellor of a major university, credited with turning the school around and raising more than half a billion dollars. His extensive network of business associates and acquaintances extended from Texas to Washington.

Montford was later appointed to the board of Atlantic Aviation, a privately held subsidiary of Macquarie Infrastructure Company (MIC).

Montford credits another relationship for landing the first in a string of corporate executive leadership roles. This time, it was the 45th governor of Texas, the late Ann Richards, who introduced John during a dinner event at the old Austin Country Club to Ed Whitacre, the former chair and CEO of two well-known American brands, AT&T and General Motors, and a Texas Tech alum.

"Relationships. Relationships. Relationships," Montford is always telling me. And now he is telling you.

In retrospect, Whitacre's very first call after being selected chair of General Motors went to a man he trusted implicitly. Whitacre hired John as senior adviser for government relations and global public policy at General Motors. It is further proof of the power of a single board appointment from the organization's perspective.

Straight Talk: Make a good first impression.

The straight truth is that every person privileged to be invited to serve on a board follows a unique path to that opportunity and brings his or her own distinct set of experiences, values, credentials, and motivators to the boardroom.

If you already serve on a board, you know this to be true. If you are one of the few to get the call, congratulations. Go celebrate, but be prepared to roll up your sleeves and contribute to the better good in the ways only you can.

If you are among the many more successful leaders who have not yet gotten the call to the boardroom, we sincerely hope that the guidance we have offered here helps you obtain that invitation to serve.

Of course, if you are called to serve on a board, it is not only important to make a good first impression. Remember, showing up is half the job. Showing up prepared is the other half.

Be sure to balance your early tenure on the board with equal parts of active listening and purposeful inquiry that leaves most of the talking to the very peers who will be evaluating your early days on the board.

Don't talk too much, too early. You have to earn the right to get up on your soapbox. You should not be assertive unless you have the facts *and* have earned the respect of your peers.

When you are playing in the boardroom—and learning the rules of engagement or board games that happen there and provide the title for this work—it pays to be mindful that your peers want a valuable contributor, not someone who is going to be assertive before earning the social capital to do so.

Straight Talk: Remember, you have to earn your right to enter the board of directors' conversation. You must have a plan and act on that plan because board appointments are not going to fall magically out of the sky and land on your lap. If you do get the call to the boardroom, serious due diligence on your part is required to make sure it is the right board for you. And if you do join a board, you must remember that making a good first impression will provide what you need to make a greater long-term impact on the board and the organization you now serve.

Chapter 2

Putting Shareholders First . . . Not Last: The Case for Dividends and the Role of Independent Directors

In this great country, it seems that at times we are obsessed with committees. Every nonprofit, every organization, every social club, fraternity, sorority, PTA, church, Rotary, Lions Club, student council, and so on has committees, and they take many shapes and sizes.

One of the most interesting committees I encountered in my career was when I was serving as chancellor of the Texas Tech University System. As some have observed, Texas Tech has one of the "neatest" college mascots in America, one known as the "Masked Rider." A student is picked each year to ride a handsome black steed; the rider is adorned with a mask, hat, and cape to resemble the infamous "Zorro." At the beginning of each game, the "Masked Rider" now gallops full steam across the gridiron to fire up the crowd.

Well, it happened at a home game in Lubbock in 1994, well before I became chancellor. Texas Tech was playing New Mexico, it was in the third quarter, and Tech had just scored. Right then, as the story goes, the cinch in the mascot's saddle was too loose, the saddle got crossways, and the horse panicked, threw off its Masked Rider, and ran up the stadium ramp, meeting an untimely death when it ran headlong into a concrete wall.

Even though Texas Tech won the game against New Mexico, this event sent such shockwaves through the Tech community that then–Tech president Bob Lawless banned future running of the mascot, being rightfully concerned about student safety and animal welfare.

Several months passed and it was decided to create a committee to deal with the "temporarily suspended from running" mascot. The horse was replaced and a new rider was selected the following year, but the mascot was not allowed to run because of the moratorium the committee put in place. This committee, known as the Committee for the Masked Rider, met for several months. It consisted of approximately twenty people, primarily faculty advisers and students.

In 1996, I was appointed by the board of regents to be chancellor of the Texas Tech University System. I felt that my shareholders, the Raider Nation, as well as the board, wanted the horse to run again.

I attended a meeting of the solemn Committee for the Masked Rider and pleaded my case, requesting that the horse be allowed to run at the opening of the game when the teams took to the field but not necessarily after each Tech touchdown, which I felt was a reasonable compromise.

After hearing my plea, the committee went into executive session. After a lengthy deliberation, the committee chair came out in the hall and advised me that the committee had voted and the horse was not going to be allowed to run.

To which I replied, not being a steward of good governance at the time, but exercising my prerogative as chancellor (CEO of the system) and recognizing the clamor of my shareholders, the Raider Nation, "This committee is dissolved."

The horse ran in the next game when Texas Tech played and beat Baylor 45–24 in front of a crowd of about 50,000 spectators who erupted with applause when the horse and its Masked Rider took the field.

Although this experience was not necessarily carried out in the spirit of democracy, it did point out that we are a nation of committees and that effective governance occasionally requires taking the pulse of your stakeholders. Since then, let me tell you, I have learned that serving on a committee of the board of directors of a publicly traded company is a much more serious matter.

Looking back on that decision at Tech, I felt that I was putting my shareholders first—the students, the alumni, the parents and grandparents. These were my stakeholders, my shareholders, I reminded myself. It was time to follow my shareholders. Even the board of regents wanted the horse to run again. After it was all said and done, the horse ran, we won the game, and I really felt that I had put my shareholders first.

Straight Talk: If you are truly committed to protecting shareholder interests, you cannot allow your board or advisory board to be held captive by committee, particularly one that is out of touch with what your stakeholders want.

TODAY'S GOVERNANCE CHALLENGE

Congratulations to you if you have been selected to serve as a member of the board of directors of a publicly listed company. Chances are, you were successful and display a level of competence and talent that your advocates felt would add value to an enterprise.

For-profit board service is, in part, a fulfillment of the American dream. You are now part of a business that exists to make a profit and create value for shareholders. You will also be compensated for your service as a director, and that brings me to another point—making a profit is not un-American and it is not a concept for which you ever need to apologize as long as your company is doing it legally and ethically.

The profit motive has long differentiated our U.S. economy from many other economies around the world, particularly those where dictators, despots, or warlords rule or where it is thought government can do it better, which seldom produces an improved economy.

In the United States, we are blessed to exist in a free enterprise system where we can, through our own ingenuity and entrepreneurial drive, make money and in the case of board service, make money for our shareholders.

If you are new to the boardroom, we hope your commitment will provide insight and oversight for the organization.

The pace of change in today's global business environment is unprecedented, as are the number and complexity of challenges faced by today's boards of directors. The risks also are higher than we have previously known, be they related to fiduciary responsibilities, financial controls, system-wide risk management, cybersecurity, or ethical and code of conduct issues.

As this chapter will confirm, there is much to consume the focus and attention of the individual director in our times. There is also an incredible, continuous flow of major priorities that seem to populate the board agenda before a meeting of directors is even scheduled. So it would be understandable if, at times, you feel swept away by the riptide of pressures and programs for which you have signed on.

Despite all of this information, much of which will be related in this and other chapters, there is really only one thing that should keep you awake at night. Not every night, just often enough to keep you connected to what is really important. That is—you are an independent director and as an independent director you represent your shareholders—the pension plans, partnerships, financial institutions, corporations, and individual investors. All of these entities have risked their money to invest in your company. Never forget it.

By being independent as a director, you can still be a team player and focus on the company's success and profitability. You do not have to be an obstructionist. You should not hesitate to speak out when you feel your shareholders' interests are not being considered or protected. Independence is not a license to obstruct. It is a motivation to contribute to the company's success.

There is one more edict that needs to be mentioned.

A source of great irritation is for a director to be absent from committee or board meetings. Like attending class in college, being present and participating in the corporate governance process is essential for the company to be governed and overseen by independent directors.

If you are not going to attend meetings, at least arrange to call in by phone and conference for the proceedings.

It seems that any director who takes his or her board service seriously has a fiduciary responsibility to *show up*.

Several years back, a Southwest Airlines director called in for a board meeting from MD Anderson Hospital in Houston, Texas, where she was undergoing a chemotherapy treatment. This truly reflects dedication above and beyond the call of duty. All other excuses for absence seem pale compared to what this director went through to call in for the board and committee meetings that day.

So, remember you serve for the benefit of the shareholders. Stay connected and participate in the board process to protect their interests.

PUTTING SHAREHOLDERS FIRST

Straight Talk: The essence of board service comes down to one direct question: What are my ethical and legal duties, as a member of the board, to act in the best interest of the shareholders I represent?

This is the essence of fiduciary responsibility and should be your guiding principle as a director.

Serving on the board of a publicly listed company is much different today than it was in times past. It is an honor to serve today, but board posts are far from honorary positions. One has serious fiduciary responsibilities as a director.

Following the accounting scandals at Tyco, WorldCom, Enron, and Arthur Andersen, there is heightened scrutiny of boards of directors as well as management for American public companies. Some of the governance changes are now required by local or state laws and regulations. However, the most significant changes in setting standards for a director's fiduciary responsibilities have been under federal law.

Straight Talk: Directors serving on boards of listed companies must possess a working knowledge of federal law and exchanges rules that govern corporate oversight by independent directors.

In carrying out your fiduciary responsibility you need to be mindful of the various legal governance and disclosures required under federal law, federal regulations, and those regulations promulgated by the listing exchanges, namely the New York Stock Exchange or the NASDAQ Global Market.

These requirements are found primarily in the following:

1. The Securities Exchange Act of 1934 as amended, known as the Exchange Act

2. The Sarbanes-Oxley Act of 2002, as amended, known as SOX

3. The Dodd-Frank Wall Street Reform and Consumer Protection Act of 2010, known as Dodd-Frank

4. The regulations promulgated by the U.S. Securities and Exchange Commission, known as the SEC

5. The corporate governance standards of the New York Stock Exchange (NYSE) and the National Association of Security Dealers Automated Quotations (NASDAQ)

6. Regulations issued by the Commodity Futures Trading Commission, known as CFTC, which are generally applicable to financial institution boards[1]

These enactments have been largely in response to various economic crises, corporate scandals, and consumer losses, which occurred beginning with the stock market crash in 1929, heightened during the corporate scandals before the turn of the century, and were amplified by the pyramid schemes, insider trades, and other bogus investor scams in the first decade of this century.

For companies listed on the exchanges, these standards were designed to hold management and directors accountable for their conduct in publicly traded companies. Boards are required to be governed by "independent" directors. Candor and transparency in financial disclosures are emphasized and designed to protect not only the company's shareholders but also the public in general. These standards require transparency and integrity in financial reporting.

This chapter will discuss these various changes, particularly as to how they underscore the fiduciary responsibilities of a director to ensure compliance and to ensure the protection of the interests of the shareholders.

THE ROLE OF THE INDEPENDENT DIRECTOR

Straight Talk: The ultimate authority for corporate governance rests with the independent directors. If it does not, your listed company has a big problem.

The most important requirement relative to an organization is that "independent directors" must comprise a majority of the board.[2] An extensive review of what "independent" means is conducted in chapter 5. Sometimes referred to as "outside" or "nonmanagement" directors, the independent directors must meet in regularly scheduled executive sessions with a nonmanagement director presiding.[3]

Here, it is important to note that one can be a "nonmanagement director" and still not qualify as an "independent director" under NYSE and NASDAQ Rules. This is because these directors may have some other affiliation or arrangement with the company that precludes them from being qualified as "independent."

The residual power of governance should rest ultimately in those directors who are independent. Independent directors can make decisions relative to corporate governance, when it becomes necessary to override the decisions of management, particularly when those independent directors act in the best interest of the shareholders. They have the power to keep management in check when it comes to possible infractions of compliance standards.

INDEPENDENT COMMITTEES

Straight Talk: Independent directors must control the Audit, Compensation, and Nominating/Governance Committee functions of the corporate board.

All publicly traded NYSE companies must have at least three committees—Audit, Compensation, and Nominating/Governance. Under NYSE Rules, many of which have been adopted by the SEC, each of these committees must consist entirely of independent directors.[4] Similar requirements exist under NASDAQ Rules, except that a majority of all independent directors must have oversight over executive compensation.[5]

The Audit Committee

All publicly listed companies must have an Audit Committee of the board of directors, and it must consist *entirely* of independent directors and have at least three members. These independent directors must meet the requirements of Section 301 of SOX, relating to independence, and Rule 10 A-3(6)(1) of the Exchange Act. The committee must contain at least one designated "financial expert" under SEC regulation S-K and if not, why not.[6]

The committee has many other functions, including the sole responsibility for appointing, compensating, or terminating the company's independent auditors as well as oversight responsibility over the company's internal auditors.[7]

Suffice it to say, as discussed later in chapter 8, service on the Audit Committee is very serious business. A host of other committee responsibilities are also discussed.

The Compensation Committee

The Compensation Committee of the board is responsible for evaluating and making recommendations to the full board for the pay and benefits for senior-level management.[8]

In addition to the Audit Committee, any publicly listed company must also have a Compensation Committee, composed only of independent directors. This means that such directors must be independent in terms of compensation. Aside from receipt of fees for serving as a director, considerable scrutiny is required for independence. Independence is questioned if such director receives any other compensation or fee paid by the company or paid to a relative of the director. In making the determination of "independence" in order to be considered independent for service on the Compensation Committee, the entire board must consider whether a director has a relationship to the company.[9]

Thus the board must determine, for independence, whether any relationship is material to a director's independence from management. In so doing the board must examine:

1. The source of any compensation a director receives for consulting or advisory fees and whether the director receives compensation from any person or entity that would impair his or her judgment about executive compensation, and

2. Whether the director is affiliated in any way with the company, a subsidiary, or an affiliate of a subsidiary company, and if so, whether such relationship places the director under direct or indirect control of the company or its senior management. The board must also consider whether there is a direct relationship between the director or senior management of such a nature that it would impair their ability to make independent judgments about executive compensation.[10]

The Compensation Committee must also have a written charter outlining the committee's responsibilities, including:

1. Setting goals and objectives for CEO compensation
2. Evaluating the performance of the CEO
3. Determining CEO compensation levels based on such evaluations
4. Making recommendations as to non-CEO executive compensation
5. Publishing a "compensation discussion and analysis" report for inclusion in the annual 10-K report[11]

The committee charter must also address an annual evaluation of the committee.[12]

Significant rights and responsibilities must also be addressed in the charter. These include:

*   That the committee has the sole right to retain and pay a compensation consultant, provided that the consultant meets the "test of independence" from management as found in NYSE Rules

*   That the committee has the sole right to retain and pay legal counsel, provided such counsel is independent from management and meets the same test for independence under NYSE Rules as the compensation consultant[13]

Also, the charter must specify the number and qualifications for members of the committee, as well as procedures for appointment and removal.[14]

Lastly, the Compensation Committee's charter should be posted on the company's website.[15]

Like service on the Audit Committee, service on the Compensation Committee of the board is very busy and time-consuming work. It requires independent oversight and monitoring of executive compensation to be effective in protecting the shareholders' interests.

The Nominating/Corporate Governance Committee

The third committee of the board required by NYSE Rules is the Nominating/Corporate Governance Committee. Like the Audit and Compensation Committees, the Nominating/Corporate Governance Committee must consist entirely of independent directors.[16]

This committee is the core committee to ensure that a charter is in place for good governance. The charter must provide guidance in a number of areas including the following:

1. Identifying qualified candidates for board service
2. Recommending nominees for board service to shareholders for the next annual meeting
3. Recommending corporate governance guidelines
4. Overseeing evaluations of the board and management together with an annual evaluation of the committee[17]

The committee charter should also address committee membership and removal, and committee operations. The charter retains in the committee the sole authority to engage and pay a search firm to find director candidates.[18]

As with the Audit and Compensation Committees, the Nominating/ Governance Committee must be included in the company's website, which must be referenced in the 10-K filing or proxy statement.[19]

NASDAQ Rules for the committee are not as rigid in some respects but do require that independent directors carry out most of the functions outlined above.

Special Committees of the Board

Straight Talk: The creation of other committees by the board should be done only if there is a function or area that cannot be covered by the "Big Three" committees.

Two areas where special committees may become necessary include:

1. Public companies that engage in "swap transacting" involving derivatives as governed by the Commodity Exchange Act and the Dodd-Frank Act[20]
2. Certain risk committees responsible for enterprise-wide risk management, like nonbank financial companies under Federal Reserve Board supervision

or publicly traded bank holding companies where required by the Federal Reserve Board[21]

Otherwise, a board may create such additional committees as it deems necessary to carry out its governance responsibilities. In this connection, one must remember that additional committees require time and expense. Before a board creates any additional committees the following questions should be asked:

1. Is the creation of a new or specialized committee in the best interests of the shareholders?
2. Can the activity or subject matter for which a new committee is requested be capably handled by an existing committee of the board?
3. Will the new committee address a persistent problem that has yet to be solved by the existing committee structure?
4. Is the creation of a new committee warranted by the time and expense required to put it in place?
5. Will the new committee receive a majority vote by independent directors in order to be constituted?
6. What type of charter will be required of the new committee?

CODES OF CONDUCT AND OTHER GENERAL GOVERNANCE REQUIREMENTS

Legal and regulatory requirements dictate strong code of conduct and ethics requirements in publicly traded companies.

SOX requires companies to disclose whether or not they have adopted a Code of Ethics for the principal executive officer, principal financial officer, and controller or principal accounting officer.[22]

This Code of Ethics must include standards "reasonably necessary" to promote:

1. Honest and ethical conduct and the handling of conflict of interest situations
2. Fair, full, accurate, timely, and understandable disclosures in SEC-required reports
3. Compliance with governmental rules[23]

Furthermore, the SEC requires under Regulation S-K that the Code of Ethics be filed in the annual report or posted on the company's website, or the company must undertake in its annual report to provide copies upon request.[24]

In addition to the publication of a Code of Ethics for senior executives, both the NYSE and NASDAQ require the adoption of a Code of Business Conduct and Ethics for *directors* (emphasis added), officers, and employees.[25]

This required Code of Business Conduct and Ethics not only addresses the SOX requirements for senior management but also must address the following:

1. Conflicts of interest
2. Corporate opportunities
3. Confidentiality
4. Fair dealing
5. Protection of company assets
6. Compliance with all laws and regulations
7. Compliance with insider trading laws
8. Reporting of illegal or unethical behavior[26]

The Proxy Statement or 10-K must state that the Code of Business Conduct and Ethics is on the company's website and provide the website address. Waivers of any Code of Business Conduct and Ethics provisions may only be approved by the board or appropriate board committee.[27]

Also, in formatting the codes of conduct, under NYSE Rules, listed companies must adopt governance guidelines that address the following:

1. Director qualifications
2. Director responsibilities
3. Director access to management
4. Director access to independent advisers, if necessary
5. Director compensation
6. Director orientation and continuing education
7. Management succession
8. Annual board performance evaluations[28]

These guidelines must be on a company's website, Proxy Statement, or annual report. The location of the Code of Business Conduct and Ethics must be set forth in the 10-K filing.[29]

Lastly, these codes must have procedures for enforcement and require consistent actions against violators.

ENFORCEMENT ACTIONS, REQUIRED NOTIFICATIONS, AND AFFIRMATIONS

In today's corporate governance, serious responsibilities are imposed on senior management and boards under federal law and exchange rules. Serious consequences exist for noncompliance.

The chief executive officer must certify annually to the NYSE that he or she is not aware of any listed standards violations or must state how standards are not satisfied.[30]

Prompt notification is required by the CEO after any executive officer becomes aware of noncompliance, whether material or nonmaterial, with corporate governance listing standards. The same notification and certification requirements exist for NASDAQ companies, except the notice and certifications must be made by the company.[31]

Most importantly, in the event of a "material noncompliance," notification in the form of an SEC 8-K disclosure filing must be made. In the event that an interim change occurs relative to listing standards in board composition, independence, or any required committees, the company must submit a written affirmation within five days after such change occurs.

The company must also submit an annual affirmation within 30 days after the annual meeting with details of compliance and noncompliance with corporate governance listing standards.[32]

Sanctions for noncompliance with Audit and Compensation Committees requirements can lead to delisting, public reprimands, or suspensions—all requiring 8-K filing disclosures.[33]

Thus, as we can readily see, the federal government and the listing exchanges are serious about director, officer, and employee conduct. These built-in protections are a valuable asset for shareholders who place their trust in a company by making investments. They also put directors as well as officers and employees on notice that the highest ethical conduct is expected of them, especially when carrying out their fiduciary duties to their shareholders and the public.

PROVEN METHODS OF INCREASING SHAREHOLDER VALUE

Shareholder value is measured by corporate success—profitability, good margins, return on invested capital, and appreciation of stock value. These successes do not happen like instant coffee. They are the product of an engaged board giving shareholders effective representation, a competent management team that executes visionary strategic planning, and a well-trained, motivated workforce. When a company is functioning like a well-tuned watch, with all the components working, it should increase shareholder value. There are several ways directors can influence increased shareholder value. Here are a few time-tested methods:

1. Make sure your company is effectively managed with a visionary strategic plan—a road map to profitability.
2. Watch corporate expenses.
3. Advocate for an ambitious ROIC (return on invested capital).
4. Advocate for share repurchase.
5. Advocate for increased dividends.
6. Consider a stock split.

Keep in mind that each of these methods are serious strategic moves and require vigilance and in most cases expertise. When properly introduced and executed, they should result in increased shareholder value.

Make Sure Your Corporation Is Effectively Managed with a Visionary Strategic Plan

As you participate in board meetings, one of the first orders of business is whether or not your company has a viable strategic plan to create and increase shareholder value.

Simply stated, a strategic plan is an organization's process for planning its direction and making decisions allocating the resources to get it there. In other words, it is a roadmap to increased profitability and shareholder value.

In 2010, when Ed Whitacre became chair and CEO of General Motors, one of the first things he did was to establish a strategic plan, direct and to the point, to get the company profitable again after bankruptcy. Whitacre brought a simple but direct strategic objective to the company— "To Design, Build, and Sell the World's Best Vehicles."

This was the roadmap to the return to profitability and increased shareholder value. It was a clear mandate. Anything that did not contribute to this objective was a waste of time and corporate resources.

Directors should insist upon ambitious and concise strategic plans— otherwise you can have a company that may stay busy, but wander aimlessly, without a focus on a long-term objective.

So ask yourself: What is this company's long-term objective and what can be done in the short term to get it there?

Your shareholders deserve nothing less. The hallmark of most successful companies these days is that ones with a viable strategic plan know where they are headed. This is Step 1 in bringing about greater shareholder value.

Watch Corporate Expenses

This point may seem to be a bit timeworn, but it is worth emphasizing. Regardless of the size of a company, if directors do not keep vigilant oversight over expenses, they can get out of control. This includes oversight of management's expense accounts.

A key function of internal auditors is to examine management's expense accounts. Often, they will be surprised at what they will find. It is amazing what patterns can be seen when monitoring expense accounts—sports bars, strip clubs, escort services, expensive wines, liquors and champagnes, large dinner parties, overlapping personal expenses disguised as business promotion expenses. Those of us with years in business have seen it all. If your auditors are vigilant, it will save your company and your managers from a lot of problems. Answering to your auditors is one thing; answering to the IRS is another.

Excess expenses are a drain on profits and shareholder value. Do not underestimate the need for director oversight in this area. By the way, director expense accounts are also fair game.

The point is that if the expenditure is not necessary to enhance a company's profitability, it diminishes shareholder value. The old adage about counting paper clips to save on expenses may be a bit of an exaggeration, but in principle it is well grounded.

Advocate for an Ambitious ROIC—Return on Invested Capital

Shareholders, particularly institutional investors, want a measured return on their corporate investments. That is one of the reasons they buy shares of stock in the first place.

Consequently, as a director you should push for a measured target or percentage to give your shareholder investors a meaningful return on invested money. It will make the company have demonstrated value and will add value to the stock.

ROIC is a good barometer of how effectively your management team is leading the company. It is the gain on investment measured by the proceeds of the sale of the invested interest. It is a measure of how much cash a company gets back for each dollar it invests in the business.[34]

ROIC targets should be set by the board annually after consultation with management.

Return on Equity, or ROE, is expressed as a percentage and calculated by dividing net income by shareholder equity. It measures profitability by showing how much profit a company generates with the money invested in it by shareholders.

Measuring ROI and ROE with CAGR (Compound Annual Growth Rate) will give you a good measure of year over year growth in shareholder value.

Advocate for Share Repurchase

Let us refresh memories about the stocks that shareholders buy. In spite of all the talk you hear about shares of stock in corporate America, there are basically two types of stock: (1) common and (2) preferred. By far, the greatest number of shares purchased on exchanges are common shares.

They represent ownership in a company and a claim on profits. Shareholders have one vote per share of common stock, most importantly, to elect board members at the annual meeting.

Preferred stock represents a degree of ownership but does not have the same voting powers. Normally the dividends are fixed for preferred shares. They take priority over common shares in the event of liquidation. Also, preferred shares can be repurchased by the corporation as a condition of ownership.

Share repurchase by a corporation must be authorized by its board of directors and is not a routine matter. First, it requires money to buy back the shares. Second, the company must have the cash on hand to buy back the shares.

Share repurchase is a way to increase shareholder value. It is simply the repurchase or reacquisition by a company of some of its outstanding shares.

It is a more flexible way to increase shareholder value than dividends. It also has the advantage of generally increasing the value of existing shares without immediate tax consequences.

SEC Rule 106–18 sets forth the requirements for a stock repurchase. A company, by rule, cannot buy back more than 25 percent of the average daily volume of shares traded.

Share repurchases occur through several methods. By far, the open market method is used the most.

In the open market method the company announces the repurchase of shares on the open market and has the option of deciding when and how many shares to repurchase, subject to the 25 percent daily limit.

Prior to 1981, tender offers were executed using a fixed price specifying the number of shares to be purchased and a stated time period within which the repurchase occurred.

After 1981, companies could use the "Dutch auction" tender offer that specifies a price range within which the share will ultimately be repurchased. Shareholders may tender their stock at any price within the range. The company tallies the various tenders and buys back the shares at the lowest price at which it can acquire the number of shares it seeks to buy back. The firm pays that price to all investors who tendered at or below that price.

If more shares are tendered than were sought to be repurchased, then the company purchases less than all the shares tendered on a pro-rata basis to those tendering at or below the purchase price.

In summary, as one can see, share repurchase is not a simple procedure but is an effective method to increase shareholder value, particularly when the share price is considered low.

Advocate for an Increase in Dividends

Dividends are simply payments to shareholders out of a company's earnings.

They vary extensively from company to company. The amount of the dividend paid is set by the board of directors.

It stands to reason that if you are representing the interests of your shareholders, you need to ensure they are paid dividends commensurate with the company's earnings. Determining a fair amount for dividends is not an exact practice. There are many corporate expenses and needs that have to be fairly addressed along with setting the amount for dividends. A true measure of corporate earnings should take into account all of the reasonable and necessary costs for running and sustaining a profitable business. That being said, dividends should be paid from earnings, and if a company is making a profit, reasonable dividends must be considered each quarter to guarantee a respectable return of earnings to its owners—the shareholders.

Straight Talk: If your company has significant earnings, as a director, you should advocate for a reasonable return through dividends. However, if your company cannot meet all dividend payments through earnings, consider a lesser amount. Selling corporate assets to pay dividends raises a red flag on shareholder value.

Many companies stake a lot of their reputation on the consistency of their dividends. When a company has to sell assets to make consistent dividend payments, this should raise a red flag to you as a director. Obviously you have a fiduciary responsibility to your shareholders, but that does not mean you have the responsibility to drive the company into the ground by voting for dividends the company simply cannot afford.

Dividends are a good measure of shareholder value if they are reasonable and affordable. It sometimes becomes a balancing act between shareholder value and corporate solvency. This is where your leadership as a director will require continued vigilance. You must make the judgment call on affordable dividends, stopping short of payments to shareholders the company simply cannot afford.

Stock Splits

A stock split occurs in a publicly traded company when the board of directors votes to increase the number of shares that are outstanding by issuing more shares to its current shareholders.

The board should consider a stock split when shares are selling at a high price and the company's financial position is strong. Liquidity is one of the most important considerations in this investment decision that a board should consider. A stock split can lower the market price of shares, resulting in increased marketability.

While there is no specific formula for a stock split, a split in the ratio of at least two shares for one seems desirable. If current and anticipated financials are good, including operating results, and earnings, dividends, book value, and revenues are strong, directors should consider a split for the benefit of the shareholders. If strong financials and anticipated growth do not warrant a two-to-one split, the board should evaluate whether or not a split is advisable. For NYSE companies, stock splits are governed by Rule 703.01 (Part 1). For NASDAQ companies, see the *NASDAQ Continued Listing Guide*, "Stock Splits," at listingcenter .nasdaq.com.[35]

Chapter 3

The Hide and Seek Game of Corporate Finance: Understanding Balance Sheets and Corporate Economics

Accounting principles in corporate America today are a complex matrix of line item entries. They have evolved from congressional and regulatory enactments that are so onerous and complex that, at times, only accountants can understand them.

The spirit of all these changes was to protect investors. The result has been to cost companies (and shareholders) a whole lot of money for compliance.

Somehow, our accounting system has gotten off track. Perhaps it came to a head with the enactment by Congress of the Sarbanes-Oxley Act of 2002 (also called "Sarbox" or SOX), which exacerbated accounting costs for corporate America.

The point is that you cannot legislate against all corporate misconduct. Sarbanes-Oxley was passed largely as a reaction to the Enron scandal of the 1990s. That episode was caused by fraudulent "off balance sheet" transactions and misrepresentations. There were plenty of laws to protect against that conduct on the books at the time. Now, we are saddled with a mirage of new regulations and practices that have cost corporations millions if not billions of dollars to achieve conformity.

All this being said, directors still have to be able to navigate this mess of facts and figures in what amounts to a game of financial "hide and seek." Wouldn't it be crazy if everybody on a corporate board had to be an accountant? Forget independence, we would all be slaves to the rules and numbers.

Here is an example of what we're talking about.

A review of several recent quarterly corporate press releases on earnings resulted in "earnings" or "income" being characterized as follows:

Gross Income

EBITDA (Earnings Before Interest, Taxes, Depreciation, and Amortization)

Operating Income

Net Income

Net Income Excluding Special Items

Net Income with Unfavorable Special Items

Net Income with Favorable Special Items

Operating Revenues

Total Operating Revenues

Comprehensive Income

Condensed Consolidated Statement of Comprehensive Income

Free Cash Flow (FCF)

Trying to understand all this financial "wizardry" takes real diligence and expertise on the part of any conscientious director. To modify a catchy phrase, "Show me the bottom line!" Is this company making money or not?

By applying a few fundamental principles, one can work through this camouflage of accounting language and get a pretty good idea of where things really stand financially. Here are a few basic principles that might help you sort out this hide and seek game of corporate finance:

1. Basic household math—In your quest for the bottom line, in order for any business to be profitable, it must have more money coming in than going out.

2. GAAP accounting or "Generally Accepted Accounting Principles" is the standardized set of accounting guidelines imposed on companies and is the required method, with a few exceptions, for reporting to the U.S. Securities and Exchange Commission (SEC).[1]

3. Corporate accounting and financial reporting is done on a three-month quarterly basis covering Q1, Q2, Q3, Q4, and on an annual basis, culminating with the filing of a 10-K or annual report with the SEC.[2]

4. Comparisons of "profits–losses" are generally done with the same quarter of the previous year, or other quarters, or on a yearly basis called YOY (Year over Year). A corporation can still be making a profit but performance can be characterized as a loss when compared to a previous quarter a year earlier or when comparing a year to a previous year.

5. Financial controls are supposed to be in place that set off alarms to management when performance or yields are not going right.

6. A balance sheet is merely an equation of how the assets in one column equal the liabilities in the other. The ownership of the corporation by shareholders or "shareholder's equity" is termed a liability as distinguished from an asset.[3]

7. Look for cash or cash equivalents and the ratio of cash to liabilities.

8. Watch out for intangibles like goodwill and other "imaginary numbers" and how they are computed. These could come back to bite if you're not diligent about oversight.

9. Take a careful look as to what percentage of liabilities consists of shareholder equity. The larger percentage, the better.

10. Get acquainted with your internal and your independent auditors.

By applying these basic principles, you as a responsible board director can begin your own, impartial quest to find the bottom line or the real financial condition and financial strength of a publicly held corporation.

Taking it just a step further, let's examine the corporate balance sheet, the consolidated statement of cash flow, the consolidated statement of expenses, shareholder equity, and, perhaps most importantly, the cash or cash equivalents on hand.

A few basic accounting practices must first be understood as we begin our analysis.

GAAP is the standardized guideline for reporting. This simply means Generally Accepted Accounting Practices. When GAAP is not being used or calculations deviate from GAAP characterization, the financials will note, for instance, "non-GAAP income" or "non-GAAP earnings." This means that the company is assessing earnings that fall outside the normal accounting definitions of income like specialized earnings from a cash investment.

Just consider free cash flow or FCF for short, which is a measure of how much cash a company generates after accounting for capital expenditures such as buildings or equipment. This cash can be used for expansion, developing new products or research, paying dividends, reducing debt, buying back stock, or other purposes.

Free cash flow measures a company's ability to generate cash. It is also a matter of special interest to some investors who believe cash flow is a more telling barometer of corporate financial health than more traditional readings such as earnings per share (EPS).

For example, to determine free cash flow, if Company ABC's cash flow statement reported $25 million of cash from operations and $10 million of capital expenditures for the year, then Company ABC's free cash flow was $25 million minus $10 million, leaving us with $15 million of free cash flow.

It is important to note, however, that free cash flow is derived from a company's cash from operations, which itself is heavily influenced by its net income.[4] That's important because whenever significant gains or expenses such as one-time gains or asset sales are logged that are unrelated to the company's core business, analysts, investors, and corporate directors alike would be well served to exclude those anomalies from their free cash flow calculations so they clearly see the company's typical cash-producing capacity.

Thus, in many instances, by applying the rigid GAAP accounting practices, a company may not show an accurate picture of earnings, as it can with non-GAAP reporting of earnings. Corporate financials will clearly state this when applying non-GAAP earning measures.

One important thing to note about non-GAAP accounting that directors must be mindful of is that management will often use non-GAAP accounting methods to compute bonuses and executive pay. This is because nonstandard accounting measures can result in greater percentages and higher yields.

This financial chicanery has become somewhat of a common practice with many companies today, and although it is not illegal, it certainly is misleading.

The next time you review executive compensation as a director, ask your compensation advisers if management's computations are based on non-GAAP accounting. If so, the complete picture needs to be presented to the board as to which accounting methods were used before any board approvals of executive pay are granted.

Public companies report their financial performance by quarters, called the "10-Q," for Q1, Q2, Q3, Q4, with the last quarter of the year embodied in an annual report of financial performance filed with the SEC called the "10-K."

It is important that directors fully understand this reporting system with the SEC because comparisons of financial performance are usually done by quarters with a look back at the same quarter's performance the preceding year, or year over year—a look back at how the company performed financially in the preceding year.

The 10-Q reports known as the "Q" must be filed with the SEC within 40 to 45 days after the last day of the fiscal quarter. The 10-K, or "K" as it is often referred to, must be filed within 60, 75, or 90 days after the end of the fiscal year, depending on the classification category of the filer.[5]

There are two other reports that directors must be knowledgeable about: the "8-K" and "Reg FD," which is shorthand for Regulation Fair Disclosure.

The 8-K is a report that companies must file with the SEC in the event that a material, often unscheduled corporate event occurs that shareholders should know about. For examples, consider the unplanned departure of a key executive (such as the CEO), a change of accounting firms, a bankruptcy filing, or the announcement of a new business deal or partnership.

Whatever the newsworthy or "shareholders should know" stimulus, the SEC requires disclosure within four business days of the occurrence of said material event.[6]

A Reg FD public disclosure is required when a selective disclosure is made of material nonpublic information. Reg FD will be discussed in greater detail in chapter 8.[7]

The upshot of all of these filings is that as an independent director searching for the bottom line, you need to learn to compare monthly, quarterly, and annual financials. This information is or should be readily available to you as a director, to your shareholders, and to the public.

One other concept to which directors need to pay special attention, and which is the subject of considerable discussion in boardrooms and accounting circles, is whether the SEC should at some point adopt a set of international financial reporting standards (IFRS), which would attempt to bring about globally applied, standardized accounting principles for companies worldwide.[8]

To date, this has been largely in the discussion stage, but ultimately its adoption could simplify financials on a global reporting basis for multinational corporations. These standards would vary from GAAP in some particulars but will require significant world diplomacy to be implemented.

With the passage of Sarbanes-Oxley in 2002, another significant change was required in that companies had to put in place financial controls that alert management and ultimately the shareholders with a system of alarms when yields on financial performance indicators are not going right.

These controls are normally embedded in software systems that notify management of problems or significant changes in financial barometers like cash flow or expenses. These controls amount to a high-tech "tickler file" that records visual alarms when things aren't going right with some aspect of corporate finances.

These days, a conscientious director needs to be knowledgeable about the concept of financial or fiscal controls that must be in place to monitor material changes in financial performance.

As you compare latest quarters to prior quarters in previous years or year-over-year comparisons (YOY), it is important to note that a corporation can still be making a profit while performance is character-ized as a loss because it is less than earnings in the same period of the previous year. This characterization seems a bit unfair at times but its effects certainly keep management and the board vigilant on trends.

With a grasp of all of these "bells and whistles"—the fundamentals of today's corporate accounting and finance—let's now take a look at some specific things:

1. Cash or cash equivalent on hand, that is, "Show me the money"
2. Cash flow
3. Expenses and liabilities
4. Shareholder equity

It should not be any secret to you as a director that the amount of cash or cash equivalents that a corporation has on hand is the strongest indi-cator of the financial strength of a company. There is no magic to this. It is just like your household accounting.

From the standpoint of ongoing transactions, is more money coming in than going out? To be a good corporate director, you have to ask yourself this important question time and again. (Apparently, to be elected to the United States Senate or House of Representatives in far too many states and districts, your task is to avoid the unpleasant implica-tions of this somehow politically charged question in the first place.)

Thus, in our quest to find the bottom line, let's first consider the cor-porate balance sheet. A sample corporate balance sheet can be found in Appendix II. Here, we will always find two columns—one for assets and one for liabilities. The balance sheet, in reality, is just a simple equation, that the assets equal the liabilities. The important thing to note here is that the shareholder equity—the value of the shareholders' ownership of the company—is included in the liabilities column.

Most everyone understands what is meant by "equity" in your home—the difference between the market value (the price you could sell it for) and what you owe against it (your mortgage). So, if you sell your home for $500,000 and you owe $300,000 on your mortgage, your equity is $200,000. On a corporate balance sheet, if you take the value of the as-sets and subtract all the liabilities except the shares owned by sharehold-ers, the net is the value of the shareholders' equity or the net amount owned by the shareholders.

"Shareholders" come in all shapes and sizes. Included in the mix you will find institutional investors, hedge funds, pension funds, other corpo-rations, and individuals. The larger the amount of shareholder equity and assets, the more value that accrues to the shareholders.

In the asset column, you should look for (1) cash on hand or readily available; (2) the status of accounts receivable; (3) investments of company cash—both short and long term; (4) intangibles—those items like goodwill that are "imaginary"; and (5) inventories and tangible property owned by the company.

No matter what any scholar tells you or what any expert on corporate finance says, the most important thing to look for on the asset side of the balance sheet equation is cash, and do not forget it! It is without question the most important indicator of the financial strength of a corporation.

Directors should also be especially vigilant of investments in derivatives. A derivative investment is one that depends on the performance of another entity—futures, options, and/or swaps. Investments in derivatives can be quite risky, so always be inquisitive about them. It's always better to ask about them lest they come back to haunt.[9]

In assessing the credibility of intangibles, one good thing Sarbanes-Oxley did was require a method by which to compute the fair value of an asset including those that are "imagined" and require valuation methods that are quite subjective.

As you gauge the strength of the asset base of a company, look carefully at the comparisons with prior months, quarters, and years. This helps determine if the company is a consistent performer.

The liabilities column sets forth what the corporation owes over and above the amount owned by the shareholders. These include hard numbers like promissory notes, accounts payable, and taxes-deferred obligations. Just like examining the assets, directors should look for the status of accounts payable and whether the company is current on its liability payments on short- and long-term debt and taxes.

It is always advisable to inquire about any contingent liabilities when examining a balance sheet. For instance, is the company involved in any protracted or expensive litigation? What is management's and legal's assessment about the probable outcome of the case?

So, does all of this diligence lead us to the bottom line? Not yet—we still need to examine the Consolidated Statement of Comprehensive Income and the Consolidated Statement of Cash Flow.

As we conclude the discussion of corporate finances and creating clarity amid the accounting shell games, it is important that directors gain familiarity with the Consolidated Statements of Comprehensive Income and Cash Flow.

Whereas the balance sheet tells us how much cash is readily available, these statements found in the monthly reports and the "Q" give us a comparison of how the corporation is faring on cash coming in and expenses going out.

These line items chart a more comprehensive look at where the income is coming from and some specifics on expenses. The "Q" charts this information on a quarterly basis as well as cumulatively up to the date totals for the year. It also gives year-over-year comparisons. Items that are in parentheses record a loss or decline in income or cash flow from prior periods.

In your search for cash and cash equivalents, the most important gauge of where the company stands is to compare the item denoted "Cash and Cash Equivalents" at the beginning of the period and "Cash and Cash Equivalents" at the end of the period.

Significant variations here should trigger questions as to which line items in this part of the report show the most variance. These cash flow changes will be picked up either from operations, investments, or financing activities. Large variations in parentheses as you look at these line items should trigger directors' questions as to "What happened here?" and "Why?"

If there is significantly less cash on hand at the end of a reporting period, directors should always ask for an explanation from management. Perhaps more than any other item, this is the real bottom line.

One final note: Since your obligation to your shareholders is a primary responsibility as a director, you should track and monitor dividend payments.

Obviously utmost consideration has to be given to a corporation's margins and profitability. However, if the dividend payments to shareholders are de minimis when compared to how much money a corporation is making, it's time for directors to step in and make sure the shareholders are getting an adequate return on their investment.

After all, the ultimate goal of any corporation is to be profitable and make a fair return to shareholders for their investment as owners. As a director, you owe it to your shareholders to ensure dividend payments represent a fair return.

Chapter 4

When Bad Things Happen to Good Boards: Protecting Shareholders and Your Reputation

In the early 1990s, while I was chair of the Texas Senate Finance Committee, I was making the rounds in Texas campaigning for reelection and visiting influential people across the state. A friend of mine got me an appointment to see Ken Lay, then the much-admired chair of then-iconic Enron Corporation, the energy, commodities, and services company based in Houston.

By that time, Ken Lay had attained corporate stardom, not just in Texas, but also across the United States. He was on just about every list of the nation's most admired chief executives then published. Lay was also well on his way to becoming one of America's highest-paid CEOs and had even served as co-chair for the organizing committee for the 1990 G8 Summit held in Houston and hosted by former president George Herbert Walker Bush.

His company, Enron, was idolized by a host of admirers and truly admired by all as a great American success story. At the time of my personal visit with Lay, holding a seat on the Enron board of directors was an opportunity to die for. Virtually any accomplished leader in the world would have leaped at the chance to be part of such a burgeoning success story. Just calling Ken Lay a friend back then would have opened innumerable doors to personal and professional networking. It did for other business, philanthropic, political, and civic leaders across Texas, and around the world.

Turns out I had a very nice visit with Ken. Actually, our meeting went so well that, surprisingly, he was moved to write me a $10,000 (wholly unsolicited) campaign check. I was flattered to have won such an impromptu endorsement from one of the most powerful corporate leaders in the world; actually, I was floored. In those days, $10,000 was a lot of money for a political donation—particularly for a state senate race, and certainly if you were from such originally humble roots as were often found in folks from West Texas.

"Gosh," I thought, "these corporate guys have a lot of money to spend!" I had enjoyed a great visit with Ken and really liked him. He struck me then as being the consummate corporate leader. I thanked him and went on my way, counting his support and the added confidence I gained from it among the many reasons I was again reelected to the Texas State Senate.

You know, looking back at that particular moment and reflecting on what might have been as well as on my years of service on the board of Southwest Airlines, I would have jumped at the chance to serve on the Enron board, as would almost any person asked before the company's disastrous unraveling. It was perceived as an iconic corporation with great leadership. After all, the company's public stock was traded on the New York Stock Exchange (NYSE), and *Fortune* magazine had named Enron "America's Most Innovative Company" for six consecutive years.[1]

Little did I or anyone else know at that time that trouble was already brewing internally with shady "off balance sheet" and "offshore" transactions. Ultimately, at the end of 2001, Enron's publicly reported financial condition was revealed to have been driven substantially by a creatively planned, systemized, and utterly institutional accounting fraud. This later led to the company's bankruptcy and, today, its infamy in American business annals.[2]

Looking back on my visit with Ken Lay, I can only count my lucky stars that Enron's leader felt nothing more than an affinity for my own personal brand of Texas politics. Boy, am I glad he wasn't compelled to think of me as a possible future addition to Enron's board, or I would have been caught up in that storm.

The lesson? Well, if you're a Texas political figure, the lesson is quite clear—beware of unsolicited campaign contributions! On a more serious note, there is something to be gleaned by today's board directors and those who aspire to board stewardship.

If we're truly honest with ourselves as leaders, we have to look back and be thankful for the things that didn't quite go our way or those instances when, for one reason or another (sheer luck, among them), purposeful meetings and conversations didn't materialize in all the ways they might have, no matter how hard we might have wished they did at the time or after the fact.

Sometimes, it is impossible to predict corporate disasters. But, quite often, there are sufficient warning signs that could alert a prospective or sitting board member to real concerns about the viability of a company on whose board he or she is considering or already serving.

Yet we can only heed these warning signs if we keep our minds open. If we ask tough questions, even if they make someone in senior management—or perhaps another member of the board—somewhat uncomfortable, we will indeed fulfill our governance responsibility to shareholders. By so doing, we will also improve our capacity to sniff out a problem, or what could escalate into a problem or even an organizational crisis, if it isn't nipped in the bud and corrected in a timely and effective manner.

Were there any such signs that Enron was in trouble?

At least at the time of my visit with Ken Lay, probably not . . . and I doubt that I would have found any had I been given reason to conduct my own due diligence on a company by whose reputation alone big business was being done and about which glowing media articles were being written. Fortunately for me, I was never asked to serve on the Enron board. But I will admit that I would have joined that board in a flash had I been offered such a directorship, which takes me back to a time in the mid-1980s when I was being sought as a director for a bank board.

TRUST IN YOUR OWN CONSCIENCE

You see, it is not hard for me to recall that earlier time in my career and that over-the-top corporate soirée I attended while being courted to join the board of a West Texas bank. After all, how many other times—then or since—have I been treated to Beluga caviar in Lubbock, Texas?

Even being considered to serve on a corporate, civic, or philanthropic board or advisory board is an honor, whether you are offered and accept the appointment or not.

To frame the occasion, I recall that in the mid-1980s, things in West Texas were going great. The oil patch was booming, real estate was high-priced, and prices for agricultural commodities such as cattle, cotton, fryers, dairy and greenhouse/nursery products, eggs and hogs were keeping lots of people in good stead.

It was in those times and amid that regional economic prosperity when an established West Texas bank in which I knew several corporate officers and board directors approached me and asked me to consider serving on its board. Wow, was I flattered! I liked the bank, I liked the officers, and I liked the directors. Check, check, and check. All the professional markers were there and they were positive.

In fact, I liked everything about the opportunity. Especially at that point in my career, I was really excited about serving on a bank's board of directors.

Subsequent to my initial euphoria, I was invited to the bank for a reception in Lubbock, known in Texas and beyond as the "Hub City" for being the economic, education, health care, and now business center of the multicounty West Texas region that is the world's largest contiguous cotton-growing region.

Well, no sooner had I arrived in Lubbock for the bank's gala reception than I was totally taken aback by what I saw. Now, mind you, I have been to a number of lavish business gatherings in the years since, replete with powerful people, exceptional food and live entertainment, and extremely interesting and compelling conversation.

Like any experienced businessman, civic volunteer, and public company board director, I have been to a lot of big, important, and memorable events in some of the finest venues in places like New York City, Los Angeles, Washington, D.C., Dallas, Houston, Paris, and London.

Yet none of these have rivaled the unbridled opulence I found myself surrounded by at this West Texas bank's gala reception in Lubbock. Much to my surprise as a then-aspiring board candidate, it was by far the most lavish party I had ever and have ever attended.

There were white-gloved waiters. Then came gobs of Beluga caviar. Partygoers sipped the most expensive champagne. Some gawked at beautiful, not overdressed young women who would make the Great Gatsby blush as they served an incredible bounty of culinary creations. You name it, this bank-underwritten party pulled out all the stops to impress not just me as a "soon-to-be member of the board," but all the other influential business, community, and political folk in attendance.

Was I impressed? Sure. You see, in our younger years, we are all more impressionable than we are later in our careers. Time and gracious mentors are, after all, great teachers. If you are not less impressionable today than you were at an earlier point in your career, you are probably not going to be an attractive candidate for any board.

But, yes, at the time, I was impressed and I was having a great time at that party. That is, until I was struck then and there by a paralyzing and career-altering thought: *Who is paying for all this?*

Sure, I knew the bank had sponsored the event. But from whose pockets was this lavish affair really being funded? The more I thought about that, the more the air gushed from the balloon—along with all my interest in serving on that bank's board of directors.

I thought to myself that an organization with shareholders who would spend this kind of money for a reception like that was simply out of control. It just did not make sense. It just did not feel right. Thankfully, that little alarm that others might call our human conscience went off in my mind and told me soon after I arrived at the party, "Something here is just not right."

A few days later, I politely declined the bank's invitation to serve on its board of directors. Looking back on what others might have then deemed a rushed and foolhardy decision at a pivotal point in my métier, I am comforted in knowing it was one of the smartest business and career decisions I ever made.

As time progressed, evidence mounted to prove my instincts had served me well. When the mid-1980s' economic bust hit the Texas real estate and oil markets, all hell broke loose. Most banks were overextended, and the jig was up. The chickens had indeed come home to roost.

Some of that bank's principals and even a few of its directors ultimately went to jail, as did numerous bankers and savings and loan executives in Texas—some of whom I am sure had attended that memorable but ultimately revealing business event in Lubbock.

The point in my retelling the story of my fateful meeting with Ken Lay of Enron and my luck at not being asked to join his board, and ultimately, my own gut decision not to join the board of that bank, is to share that if you are one of the fortunate persons to be offered a directorship, you need to exercise due diligence and carefully check out the particulars of the company with which you are about to associate yourself.

CORPORATE SOLVENCY AND YOUR REPUTATION

When you agree to join a board or advisory board, you are inexorably tying your reputation, your experience, and your good name to that of the organization, be it a global enterprise, a publicly owned company, a community or civic organization, or a philanthropic, educational, or campaign- or issue-centered body or institution.

Now more than ever before, your reputation matters, and your reputation is now reflected across an ever-widening technological and social universe that knows no horizon. There is even a cottage industry being built around so-called "reputation management." Sure, marketing and media consultants will offer to help you put your best self forward in a professional sense, helping you build the professional business network and reputation that can help you get to where you want to take your career.

But you would be wise to remember this key observation: You are the primary driver of your reputation. The way you lead and interact with and inspire others. The language you use. The decisions you make, and those you fail to make. Your commitment to listen and to learn really matters. Your character counts for a lot. Where you spend your time and with whom does, too. Your grace, concern for others, and works of charity both seen and unseen matter.

Collectively, these are the things that help build a sound reputation. And once it's sullied, it is very hard to reclaim. Just consider the people who led Enron Corporation, or the bank, savings and loan principals and directors who made a series of bad decisions that ultimately came back to haunt them and force them behind steel bars.

WHEN THINGS GO WRONG, GOOD DIRECTORS HOLD THE FORT

Inevitably, when you serve in a director's chair, you are going to walk into a board meeting or receive a frantic call about a major problem that has occurred or that is developing, stoked perhaps by a frenzy of social media and elevated to a significant organizational crisis.

Some of these problems could have and should have been prevented. In other situations, however, even the most experienced, the most prepared, and the most diligent of board members simply could not have seen it coming.

Today, truth be told, a single problem can snowball to crisis proportions because of factors that many times you have absolutely no power to control or anticipate. Often, sheer momentum and our 24-hour news cycle will enable the issue to build upon itself, multiplying the complexity of the challenge at hand and forcing the board's immediate intervention to stave off a complete collapse of the enterprise or irreversible damage to its brand identity.

Sometimes, it just happens, even to the "big boys" of corporate America.

Whether they could have been prevented or not is debatable. Consider the magnitude of corporate nightmares like the *Exxon Valdez* disaster, an ill-advised change to the legacy formula for Coca-Cola, the Tylenol poisoning, major airline bankruptcies, the firing of Steve Jobs, the collapses of Bear Stearns and Lehman Brothers, the fall of Martha Stewart, and the *Deepwater Horizon* explosion and sinking that killed 11 crewmen and caused the largest offshore oil spill in U.S. history, among many others.

The scale of these and other corporate, environmental, and in some cases, global catastrophes is today magnified simply as a function of the size, complexity, and interdependence of a global economy that is at best unpredictable. In fact, there may be no better proof of the butterfly effect than the sometimes foreseeable but often unexpected gyrations we will read about in today's business headlines.

Witness the enormous swings that can occur in stock prices and markets just because some analyst "pops off" or Jamie Dimon does not get an even bigger bonus at JPMorgan Chase. Whether they are flapping their wings or flapping their gums, individuals halfway around the world or in our own backyards can trigger market-moving events that can lead to potential governance headaches, or worse, as never before.

The point is that, as a director, you must be prepared to face the maelstrom when and if it comes. And if you have served long enough in the boardroom, you can strike the word "if" from the line above. Inevitably, crisis in one form or another will find you.

Such was the case in 2007, when I was serving on the board of Fleetwood Enterprises Inc. Serving on this board, by that time, had been one of the most enjoyable business experiences of my many careers.

Fleetwood Corporation was founded by the late John C. Crean, who basically started the business of manufacturing small recreational vehicle (RV) units and built a business that became one of the largest manufacturers of RVs in the United States. It also grew to become one of the nation's largest producers of manufactured homes.

The company's headquarters were in Riverside, California. Its shares traded on the public markets, and its name appeared in the *Fortune 500* for nearly three decades. Fleetwood was a model for board engagement.

The company's directors were highly competent and very successful businessmen and businesswomen. They brought experience and know-how in almost every aspect of business leadership—from finance, insurance, law, accounting, and transportation to investment banking, commercial markets, and higher education.

Just as important, Fleetwood's directors were exceptionally qualified and they were wholly engaged.

During the years I served as one of the company's directors, attendance at its board meetings was almost always 100 percent. The board's committees did their work diligently, in my opinion, and the board's directors were about as "hands on" as they needed to be or should have been.

Too, this board was no freshman class of directors. It was comprised of people like the late Danny Villanueva, a famed Dallas Cowboys kicker, hugely successful California businessman and investor; David Engelman, former chief operating officer of Mortgage Guaranty Insurance Corporation (MGIC), who knew corporate finance and the insurance industry as well as any business person in the country; Loren Carroll, formerly with Ernst & Young, a talented certified public accountant (CPA), who chaired the Audit Committee; Tom Pitcher, chair of the board, former commercial lawyer with the firm of Gibson Dunn and Crutcher; Margaret Dano, chief executive officer of an office supply conglomerate, and other talented directors.

These directors were hardworking, informed, and knew the RV and manufactured housing business, knew the markets, watched management's fiscal controls and handling of inventories, supply chains, and personnel. Risk management was a daily table topic.

There was continuous vigilance on cash flow and inventories. In fact, during my eight years on the board, we replaced two CEOs whose management fell short of our goals and expectations. Suffice it to say, we were fully engaged as directors.

It was an exciting business and I looked forward to each board meeting with great anticipation . . . and then, with little warning . . . disaster struck.

Some early warning signs of the "Great Recession" that was felt across the global economy beginning in 2008 actually began to hit Fleetwood right in the gut in 2007. RV sales plummeted across the country and with our inventories we had a colossal problem.

It seemed that the buying public's discretionary spending dried up almost overnight, particularly for a business that was fueled by leisure time. We were almost immediately forced to close several factories across the United States.

I can truly say that we were most fortunate to have Tom Pitcher as our board chair because he rose to the occasion and provided his usual exceptional competence and leadership. So, in spite of the economic crisis that occurred and its impact on the business, the strength of this board's character and leadership capably navigated a very tough set of facts and circumstances.

They used to ask us in the United States Marine Corps Officer Basic School, when a fire fight breaks out and all hell breaks loose, "What do you do now, Lieutenant?"

So, with that training behind me, I immediately thought, "What could we, as a responsible board of directors, do to save the company?"

Sure, what I'm about to share may not work in every emergency, but this retelling of what in retrospect seemed a purposeful, not panic-driven response to economic challenges beyond our control made the best out of a bad situation.

First, we carefully reviewed our options and, after hours of difficult meetings and tough, but straightforward discussions, we decided to file for Chapter 11 reorganization.

Second, and perhaps most importantly, we stayed engaged as a board and carefully navigated the minefields that are attendant on a bankruptcy filing and reorganization.

Third, we tried to salvage the best possible deal for our shareholders. We marshaled our assets and sold the company in four divisions to reclaim as much value as possible under the circumstances: (1) RVs; (2) manufactured housing; (3) military housing construction; and (4) Internet technology systems. We were honest and forthright in our disclosures.

Ultimately, parts of Fleetwood's former business were sold to a private equity firm and another company. Today, the legacy elements of the company do business from another part of the country, and some under other brand names.

While the Fleetwood legacy in some ways lives on, so too do the memories of an incredible company and the lessons imparted by an amazing set of boardroom peers who also became dear friends, despite how our service to the company ended.

Was that board's run through turbulent waters an enjoyable time? No, certainly not. But there are important and timeless lessons today's directors can gain from our collective experience with the Fleetwood board.

By staying engaged as a board we confronted a very difficult and almost impossible situation and made the best of it.

This whole episode was one of the most trying and disappointing episodes in my business career, but I can sleep at night knowing that as a board and as individual directors, we did everything possible to salvage a great business.

The board put our shareholders front and center of our deliberations over how to effectively re-organize so they would recoup as much of their ownership value in the company as possible.

Our reorganization of the company was handled so well from a governance perspective that the only lawsuits that resulted amounted to a few "clawback" actions against some company executives who allegedly withdrew their pensions early. All the employee pension funds were otherwise left intact.

Anyone versed in just how litigious our American business environment has become will appreciate the near impossibility of not being sued for one thing or another—whether grounded in truth or fiction—as a company is being forced into and working to recover from a bankruptcy filing.

Whether a company on whose board you serve gets sued or not, you may be seeing and hearing from a lot of lawyers anyway.

Though I can still lose sleep about Fleetwood and my board service to that stellar company, I can completely justify our conduct as directors and our dutiful handling of an economic disaster.

I am comforted to know that we, as a board, did everything reasonably possible to keep the company afloat and, only when that was no longer possible, we did the only thing we could do—and that was to effect an orderly dissolution.

The facts about Fleetwood Enterprises Inc. are a matter of public record—but what should not be lost in the annals of that company is a long record of exceptional growth, distinguished service to customers, and loyalty to shareholders in the best of times and also during the worst of times.

I still believe it was one of the best boards on which I have ever served.

In hindsight, I really loved that company. I would have bought it myself if I could have raised the funds to do so. I relate this story now because, inevitably, as a director of a major company, as a member of a civic, community, institutional, or philanthropic board or advisory board, you too must accept the reality that you could wake up one day and find yourself in the middle of a real organizational crisis.

Yes, at one time or another, you and the organization on whose board you serve may well face a crisis of some type. You may find yourself and your board prepared or completely unprepared, but remember not to rush to judgment or delay or hide from the inevitable. Information, a cool head, and a careful consideration of the potential impacts of your decision making will serve you well, but perhaps not entirely.

With this in mind, we've put together a simple but concise list of *Board Priorities for Crisis Management* that might be helpful when you and a board on which you serve are faced with such challenging circumstances.

So, when disaster strikes consider this:

Board Priorities for Crisis Management

1. Do not resign and run away from the problem. Stay focused and engaged as a board member. You cannot undo what has happened, so you will have to make the best of what could be a very bad situation.

2. Make every reasonable effort to save the business for the benefit of your shareholders.

3. Then, if all else fails, put together an exit plan including Chapter 11 or even Chapter 7 and avail your company of the lawful remedies that are available to you.

4. Pay down as much debt as possible and try to salvage the remaining assets for the benefit of your shareholders.

5. Get a communication plan that is effective, straightforward, and honest. Do not distort the facts—tell it like it is—the good news and the bad news. At all times, be honest and forthright with the media, your shareholders, employees, and all interested parties.

6. Try to salvage and protect employee pension plans and employees' vested plans. After all, they earned it, so try to keep it in place.

7. Make decisions that are informed and in good faith.

8. Secure competent outside legal help.

9. Help your management and employee teams relocate when possible and transition to new companies when part or all of a business is sold or transferred to a new company.

10. Make sure you have and maintain adequate directors and officers (D&O) liability coverage to cover situations that may arise, including a "tail" claim policy that covers future years.

    a.   And last, but not least,

11. Stay engaged as a director until the *bitter* end.

It should go without saying that, before you commit to serving on any board, you must do a lot of homework so you understand what you are signing up for and what will be expected of you as a director. Consider the points we have assembled below as something of a board service checklist.

Thankfully in this "post–Sarbanes-Oxley era," there is a treasure trove of information available for you to check out the solvency and track record of public companies. However, you need to be especially diligent when checking out private, nonpublic companies as well as the solvency, operations, and leadership of not-for-profits and other institutional boards and advisory boards because the information about these organizations, large and small, is not so readily available.

Corporate Solvency and Reputation Checklist

- For public companies, pull 10-Qs, 10-Ks, and Proxy Statements for the last five years and review them carefully.

- Do a search online to see what you can find out about the company. There is so much more information available these days, but be mindful that it's a blessing and a curse. The Internet gives everyone a voice, so be sure that whatever you're reading is from a trusted source or reflects real events, people, and issues.

- Determine whether the company has ever declared or filed for bankruptcy.

- Do a search online of the senior officers and key directors to find out all the information about them that you possibly can.

- In the United States and for companies headquartered here, check records of the U.S. Securities and Exchange Commission (SEC), the Federal Trade Commission (FTC), the Occupational Safety and Health Administration (OSHA), the National Labor Relations Board (NLRB), and other relevant federal and state agencies for any enforcement actions against the company.
- Check out the track record of the company's independent auditors.
- Check the minutes of the company's annual meeting to find out if any problems or concerns were raised.
- Check with Institutional Shareholder Services (ISS) and get whatever new information it will provide.
- Make sure the company carries good directors and officers liability insurance (D&O coverage).
- Check out the company's health care plan and try to determine how the company treats its employees.
- Check with appropriate state and local regulatory agencies about the company's reputation.
- Talk to an existing director, employee, officer, shareholder, or vendor to find out how they view the company from the inside and the outside.
- For public companies, check their NYSE or NASDAQ stock prices or those listed with other global exchanges and track the stock's performance for at least the past three years.

Once you have done all of this, you should be in a good position to move forward with your own informed decision to accept or decline an invitation for board service. You will have learned a lot about the organization and can make that decision with the confidence of knowing how your experience, skills, and values align with those of the board that wants you.

Chapter 5

Meeting Your Fiduciary Responsibility: Your Personal Declaration of Independence

Straight Talk: Independent directors should avoid any conduct or relationships that question their independence.

The need for independence, as chronicled by Thomas Jefferson in the Declaration of Independence, was firmly embedded in our history and in the culture of our country. It is reflected in the spirit of the American psyche. Americans do not like to be told by others how to run their daily lives, how to think, or how to vote. Americans like to make up their own minds about their values. They have always been, and will always be, independent thinkers.

This long-standing psyche has carried over into the governance of American corporations. By NYSE and NASDAQ Rules, the governing boards of our publicly traded companies must have a majority of "independent" directors on their boards.[1]

Not only must a listed company's board be composed of a majority of independent directors, but NYSE Rules now require that the three major committees (Audit, Compensation, and Nominations/Governance) must consist of independent directors. NASDAQ Rules require that CEO and other executive officers' compensation must be determined or recommended to the board by a Compensation Committee consisting of at least two members who must be independant directors.[2]

The insistence of requiring independent directors to control governance of the company is founded in the belief that only independent directors can protect shareholders' interests from being compromised by management. Independent directors are more likely to keep management in check and on track, preventing some of the abuses that give rise to legislative and regulatory reforms.

WHAT DOES "INDEPENDENT" MEAN?

Under NYSE Rules, an independent director is one who the board of directors "affirmatively determines" has no material relationship with the listed company either directly or as a partner, shareholder, or officer of an organization that has a relationship with the company. Some additional rules apply to membership on the Audit and Compensation Committees.[3]

The guidelines for independence are many and complex. It is necessary to discuss them in detail since board members and management need a working knowledge of their application to ensure that directors are qualified as independent.

Additional restrictions for Audit and Compensation Committee directors nullify independent status for NYSE listed company directors if the:

- Director is, or has been within the last three years, an employee of the company or an immediate family member of the director is, or has been within the last three years, an executive officer of the company.

- Director has received, or has an immediate family member who is an executive officer of the company and has received, during any 12-month period within the last three years, more than $120,000 compensation directly from the company (not including compensation received for director service, pension plan payments, or deferred compensation for prior service not contingent on continued service).

- Director or an immediate family member is a current partner of the company's Internet or external auditor; the director is a current employee of the auditor; an immediate family member is a current employee of the auditor and personally works on the company's audit; or the director or an immediate family member was within the last three years a partner or employee of the auditor and personally worked on the company's audit within that time.

- Director or an immediate family member is, or has been within the last three years, employed as an executive officer of another company where any of the listed company's present executive officers at the same time serves or served on that company's Compensation Committee.

- Director is a current employee, or an immediate family member is a current executive officer, of an organization that has made to or received from the company payments for property or services in an amount which, in any of the last three fiscal years, exceeds greater of 2 percent of such other company's consolidated gross revenues or $1 million. Charitable contributions are not considered "payments" for purposes of this prohibition but contributions meeting these thresholds must be disclosed on the company's website or in its annual proxy statement or annual report on Form 10-K.[4]

For NASDAQ listed companies an independent director is one who is not an executive officer or employee of the company and who, in the board's opinion, has no relationship that would interfere with the exercise of independent judgment in carrying out director responsibilities.[5]

Additional restrictions for Audit and Compensation Committee directors nullify independent status for NASDAQ listed company directors if the:

- Director is, or has been within the last three years, an employee of the company or an immediate family member is, or has been within the last three years, an executive officer of the company.
- Director accepts, or a family member who is an executive officer of the company accepts more than $120,000 compensation from the company during any 12-month period within the last three years (not including compensation received for director service, tax-qualified retirement plan payments, or other nondiscretionary compensation for prior services rendered).
- Director is, or a family member is, a current partner of the company's outside auditor or was a partner or employee of the company's outside auditor who worked on the company's audit at any time during any of the past three years.
- Director or a family member is employed as an executive officer of another company where any of the listed company's current executive officers during the past three years served on the Compensation Committee of such other company, or
- Director or a family member is a partner in (but not a limited partner), or a controlling shareholder or an executive officer of an organization that has made to or received from the company payments for property or services in an amount which, in the current or any of the last three fiscal years, exceeds the greater of 5 percent of recipient's consolidated gross revenues or $200,000. Charitable contributions are considered "payments" for purposes of this prohibition.[6]

Additionally, Section 301 of Sarbanes-Oxley and the SEC rule implementing this section prohibit Audit Committee members from accepting any consulting or advisory fees (other than for being a director or Audit Committee member) or to an entity in which the director is a partner, member, or principal and which entity provides accounting, consulting, legal, investment banking, financial, or other advisory services.[7]

The so-called "three year cooling-off period" applies to the foregoing "bright line" disqualification standards for both NYSE and NASDAQ companies. No individual who has any of the relationships listed within the three-year period or who is an immediate family member of an individual who had such relationships may be considered independent, even though he or she no longer has such relationships.[8]

Thus, one can lose one's classification as an independent director with family or financial relationships that do not pass the test for independence.

Most importantly, as has been and will be stated many times, independent directors *must* comprise a majority of the board.

EXECUTIVE SESSIONS

Other mandates for independent directors include the requirement that nonmanagement directors meet in executive session. NYSE Rules require "regularly scheduled" executive sessions, without management. Most boards as a matter of practice convene executive sessions during scheduled board meetings.[9]

A NASDAQ listed company's independent directors must meet in executive session without management at least twice a year.[10]

PRESIDING OR LEAD DIRECTORS

Although not referenced in NASDAQ Rules, NYSE listed companies require that a nonmanagement director must preside at executive sessions, although the same director is not required at all such sessions. The name of the director presiding at executive session or the procedure by which the presiding or lead director is selected for each executive session must be disclosed on the company's website or set forth in the Proxy Statement or 10-K filing. Also required is information about how interested parties can communicate with the presiding director or nonmanagement directors as a group.[11]

As one can see, great lengths have been taken to define what is meant by "independent director." If a board has questions about whether or not a director qualifies as independent under the foregoing rules, the board should consult with legal counsel and even outside legal counsel, if deemed necessary.

Considering the concept of independence, suffice it to say that a director should feel truly independent in his or her judgment and fiduciary responsibilities to the shareholders. A director who qualifies as independent according to regulatory definitions but is overly sympathetic to management could lose the confidence of the other members of the board as well as the shareholders. Again, the best practice for independent directors is to not get "cozy" with management but to keep your relationships founded on mutual respect and avoid any appearance of impropriety that might tarnish your reputation for independence with your board and your shareholders.

In short, here are some guidelines to maintain your independence as a director:

- Avoid financial relationships with the company you serve as an independent director on its board except for your director's fees, shares, grants earned for director service, and reasonable and necessary out-of-pocket expenses.

- Avoid situations where members of your immediate family or members of the firm where you work have a significant financial relationship with the company where you serve as an independent director.

- Avoid the appearance of any improprieties with management and employees of the company where you serve as an independent director. Substantial gifts from management to your favorite charities or organizations you are affiliated with are discouraged.

- Avoid an overly "cozy" or "fraternal" relationship with management. Keep your dealings at arm's length. There will be times when you may disagree with the course management is taking. Don't make your job of being independent more difficult. Keep your dealings with management on a high plane founded on mutual respect. Dating, romantic, or personal relationships with anyone in the company where you serve as an independent director can have serious consequences and jeopardize your independence.

Lastly, independence is a state of mind. You can still be a "team player" and be independent. It should not be a license to obstruct. Conscientious independent directors will know when they compromise their independence when they put self-interest and personal feelings above the interests of their shareholders. That is a time when one should stop, think, listen, and consider the consequences. If you feel conflicted on a particular vote of the board where your independence might be questioned, then state your conflict in open session and recuse yourself from voting. If you feel generally compromised as an independent director, it may be time to gracefully step down from board service and let someone else serve the shareholders' best interests. After all, this is the essence of fiduciary responsibility. You should know when you cross the line.

MEASURING INDEPENDENCE—BOARD SELF-EVALUATIONS

Straight Talk: Self-evaluation by your board peers can give valuable and candid insights on how effectively the board and its committees are performing.

An evolving practice to reinforce a board's independence is the practice of boards of directors periodically doing "self-evaluation" on how they are functioning as a board and how effectively the various board committees are operating.

NYSE Rules require an annual evaluation of the Audit Committee's performance. The rules also require that both the Compensation Committee and the Nomination and Corporate Governance Committee provide for annual reviews in their charters.[12]

Here are some suggestions to make board self-evaluations the most effective practice:

First, develop a series of questions soliciting candid responses from the individual board members about each committee's performance as well as that of the entire board. These questions should cover the most important responsibilities of each committee as well as responsibilities of the entire board.

Second, the questionnaire should be administered anonymously and the responses should be kept anonymous—that is important to encourage candor and frank replies in the board members' observations.

Not many directors or executives are fans of anonymous complaints. One could make the argument that a board member should possess the strength of character to "tell it like it is" and not worry about what other directors think. With the limited number of board members, normally it is not difficult to figure out who has what opinion about what is going on. That being said, the main reason to have anonymous evaluations is to create an environment of candor and take criticisms in the right vein. Is the board doing what it should be doing to advance the corporate agenda, protect the interests of shareholders, and exercise high standards of compliance? If any board member is offended by criticisms, then perhaps he or she should find another line of work.

Third, to make the practice effective, have the general counsel be responsible for administering the questionnaires, tabulating the responses, and reporting the results back to the full board. No doubt the results will eventually get back to management, so the board might want to require that the results are not for publication and cannot be disseminated until made available to the full board.

Fourth, the questionnaire should seek candid responses about how management is doing its job in carrying out its responsibilities, and in particular its relationship with the board. Every area of corporate activities and operations is fair game for periodic evaluations. Criticisms and suggested improvements should be brought to the board's attention without attributions. This is because a board should be more interested in correcting deficiencies than worrying about who is criticizing whom.

Fifth, the board should have an executive session to fully and frankly discuss the results of the survey. These responses should be vetted, particularly any written criticism or commentaries. If a committee is not doing its job or has a problem, this is the time to take corrective action and not wait until some crisis develops. Likewise, the results of the survey can be kept confidential within the board if sensitive information is contained in the responses. That being said, where a practice or omission is disclosed that could amount to a material weakness, the board must take corrective action immediately and not risk hearing the old adage, "I told you so."

Any questionnaires, to be effective, will need to be tailored to the type of business in which the corporation is engaged. A sample questionnaire for board self-evaluation is contained in Appendix III. Many sample forms can found online. Periodic self-examination is a good thing. If done regularly, they can be an excellent tool for identifying problems early and taking necessary corrective action before an event becomes a crisis.

Full transparency is the best practice. However, keep the responses anonymous since you want people on the board to bare their souls and honestly speak their minds without fear of attribution or retribution. Of course, if a material deficiency emerges in the process, it will have to be appropriately disclosed and reported.

Chapter 6

The CEO as Board Chair: How Aligning or Separating These Roles Frames the Game

Most corporate boards, at least in the United States, have a fairly standardized organization that has evolved largely through Securities and Exchange Commission requirements through the years.

There is, of course, a "chair," also referred to as a "chairman," "chairperson," or "chairwoman." The role of board chair is the subject of considerable debate when that person is also the organization's chief executive officer.

Many—including one of your co-authors here—believe that the roles of board chair and CEO should be separated with distinct lines drawn between management and the board of directors.

Some say this keeps the board more independent and that allows it to function better as the best strategic barometer for corporate performance and alignment with shareholders' ambitions. I have served on boards structured both ways and, frankly, good arguments can be made for either type of organization.

Let's first explore these:

THE CEO AS BOARD CHAIR

Strong arguments can be made that, in order for a CEO to guide a company through the contemporary morass of corporate finance and onerous regulatory requirements, the CEO should be "captain of the ship" and that means also chair of the board.

Supporters of this structural concept argue that the CEO is the person best suited to lead the corporate enterprise because he or she is ultimately responsible for its success or failure.

Critics contend, however, that when this dual alignment of the chair and CEO titles is enabled, the board is captured and apprehensive about committing to any decision or taking any position that runs counter to the wishes of the chair.

In other words, the board loses its true independence as a governing body when the chair is also the CEO. Too, the minute the CEO is the chair, the board has at least one member who will *never* be considered independent.

To be fair, let's summarize the arguments on both sides of the issue:

Corporations with the CEO Also Serving as Board Chair

Critics contend:

1. The board loses its independence.
2. The other board members can be intimidated by the presence of the CEO as chair of the oversight function.
3. The board's judgment will be "tainted."
4. The board has one less independent director.
5. A CEO who is effectively doing his or her job does not actually have sufficient time to also serve effectively as board chair.
6. The linkage of chief executive and governance duties may be viewed as a conflict with a director's fiduciary responsibilities to shareholders.
7. The critical issues of CEO compensation and succession become very clouded and a source of real sensitivity and potential conflict for board members, so the default position is often to ignore these important priorities.
8. The board chair has to ostensibly attempt to judge his or her own performance as the company's chief executive and perhaps even evaluate the strategy on which he or she has taken the lead.
9. There is simply too much authority and risk riding on the health and judgment of just one individual serving in both the CEO and board chair roles.
10. It may be more difficult to attract directors to a board whose chair is also CEO because some potential board candidates will be philosophically opposed to working with a dual CEO–board chair and won't want to be part of that dynamic, therefore limiting access to some portion of today's director talent pool.

CEO and Board Chair Separated

Critics contend:

1. One cannot serve three masters—the board, the shareholders, and employees. Thus it weakens the CEO as the company's leader.

2. There is a potentially greater risk of a fundamental disconnect between the CEO and the board of directors.

3. Divergent views on strategy and execution can impinge on the overall competitiveness and effectiveness of the enterprise.

4. It fosters too much dissension and suspicion about things that could be occurring behind the CEO's back and those of individual board directors.

5. It does not allow the CEO to fully exercise his or her leadership, often when making important strategic decisions.

6. The board still can have a majority of independent directors.

Although the NYSE (New York Stock Exchange) and ISS (Institutional Shareholder Services) frown on the chief executive also serving as chair of the board, I have served on boards that are configured both ways and frankly, effectiveness really depends on two factors as to which system works best. These are (1) leadership and (2) success.

If a corporation is functioning well, has good return on investment, and has consistently driven increases in shareholder value, why change it? You know that old saying, right? "If it ain't broke, don't fix it."

I hear from a lot of "do-gooders," if you and my esteemed co-author will pardon the expression, who think they know more than everybody else (Joe assures me this is indeed the case), generally that the chair and chief executive roles should be separate. But, if the system is working, or if it is at least enabling a company to thrive, why change it?

Southwest Airlines is a good example. The company has had 43 consecutive years of profitability, not a single layoff after 9/11/2001, and continues to thrive, not bad for a company that makes it work with 11 different employee unions!

Southwest was nurtured under the watchful eye of Herb Kelleher, one of the most brilliant CEOs in America, from whom we were honored to welcome a foreword to this book.

Herb remained president, CEO, *and* chair of the board until his retirement on June 19, 2001. He was a master at employee relations as well as governmental relations.

Herb carefully guided the company to remarkable growth and profitability through the years. Southwest Airlines stock split a remarkable 14 times. Its fleet and service areas grew at a methodical but consistent pace.

Herb knew the industry and knew the business of how to make an airline tick.

He instituted a number of changes that reflected good governance and included annual elections of board directors. He never interfered with the independent directors' ability to run the board's committees.

Herb was a strong, ethical leader, so why would anyone want to quarrel with the way Southwest Airlines was organized?

To be fair, I am using as an example one of the most successful companies in American history and an iconic American business leader as examples to illustrate my point. There are surely examples where the responsibility of juggling both the CEO's role and that of the board's chair simply proved too overwhelming, examples that do not merit retelling here.

Because many CEOs also serve as chair of company boards, what has evolved is the emergence of the "lead director."

THE LEAD DIRECTOR

The powers of the lead director are derived from the board.

The lead director presides over executive sessions as the nonchair spokesperson for the board and is generally seen as the key division between the board and the CEO and senior management.

The lead director is a key position if the individual who occupies this role is selected by the board via an independent vote, and not just "named" by the CEO.

It is also important that the lead director be on the Executive Committee and even be chair when serving with the CEO–board chair on his or her Executive Committee. The Executive Committee is empowered to act on the board's behalf in certain instances where that authority is delegated and authorized in the bylaws of the corporation.

> **Straight Talk:** When the Executive Committee takes an action that is subject to the governance requirements of federal law and rules of the NYSE and NASDAQ, care must be exercised that the decision is made by a majority of independent directors on the committee.

Now, I have to again stop and consider what my co-author Mr. McCool has seen and experienced. This is clearly Joe's turf, and it is only right in our unique spirit of Texas and spirit of New Hampshire partnership that I take my occasional lumps on issues related to board succession and board recruitment and how they relate to this critical issue of separating the roles of CEO and board chair.

Joe has indeed seen cases where companies (including clients of The McCool Group) have successfully aligned the CEO and board chair roles with tremendous effect across a variety of industry spaces.

He has also witnessed how the combination of those roles can fundamentally limit the board's authority, candor, collaboration, and overall thinking. In these instances, the elephant in the room is an untouchable topic. The combination of the CEO role with that of the board chair too often leads to insulation, cronyism, and too many directors going along to get along.

In Joe's experience and estimation, it is for organizations that combine the most visible and powerful roles that the biggest risks and surprises loom.

Besides, he points out, the responsibilities for both the CEO and the board chair have, if anything in recent years, multiplied in scope and scale, making it harder to convince anyone on the outside—shareholders included, in some instances—that adequate time and attention is being paid to both roles unless one of them is taking a clear back seat to the other.

Just do the math. Consider the 50-, 60-, and 70-hour workweeks that many chief executives must work to achieve their strategic objectives. Add to that number the hundreds of hours per year that may be required to conduct the board's business and, no less, construct and prepare for board meeting agendas. When you do the math, it becomes harder to see the combination of the CEO-chair roles being a truly sustainable model.

One must also factor in the question of CEO succession. In fact, board directors must do much more than that if they are to lead and meaningfully contribute to the task of hiring (and firing, if need be) the chief executive, which Joe has affirmed and countless directors have agreed ranks as Job #1 for all directors.

If the roles of CEO and board chair are combined, McCool asserts, what most often results is a lack of focus on CEO succession planning because the topic makes directors uncomfortable talking about the "what if's?" related to their current board leader *and* management leader.

The dialogue about succession planning, as a result, often goes something like this: "Well, I think we'll have Jim or Tom or Cathy as long as he or she is inclined to stay." That makes directors seem meek and subservient. It can also leave them totally flat-footed in times of crisis.

Yet what really is needed is an ongoing process for performance evaluation of the CEO, which of course ties quickly to compensation, and also serious board discussion about corporate strategy, the health of the organization (financially and culturally), and its future strategic investments.

With the CEO also serving as board chair, even if there is a lead director on the board, this focus may become diluted and meaningful conversation muted by the social norms that are often driven by dual titling of the CEO and board chair.

Now Joe would be the first to tell you that if a company has a track record of success, so long as directors are proactively minding their CEO succession options and aligning those with their chair's desire to lead senior management, companies need not change for change's sake. If the shareholders are on board with the dual responsibilities being left to one individual, that is their purview.

But the clear and mounting inertia is, without doubt, swinging in favor of separating the CEO and board chair roles for many of the reasons we outlined to start this important chapter.

At a time when risk management is a critical concern not only for boards but also for senior management in companies and not-for-profit and institutional boards, too, succession and leadership risks must also be evaluated along with the organization's preparedness in the event that disaster strikes.

It should go without saying that companies and directors with a dual CEO–board chair should be proactively leading on CEO search and succession planning. Yet most are not. That, friends, is a real red flag and one that even the best-performing companies cannot reasonably defend.

That is quite often because serious thinking and discussion of those priorities would make that individual leader uncomfortable, and the go-along to get-along types on the board don't want to ruffle anyone's feathers, let alone the CEO and chair.

And let's face it. There is a real risk of that happening when one considers that some leaders are actually intimidated by the matter of succession. Their ego and need, at all times, for self-preservation inhibits their own serious consideration of who would succeed them, so the issue goes by the wayside.

Great leaders create their own succession plans. Many other "leaders" are intimidated by the task and are really only standing in the way when it comes to planning for the future, aligning talent to organizational strategy, and reducing risks that could jeopardize shareholder returns.

YOUR CHALLENGE AS A DIRECTOR

Whatever side of this issue you, as a director or would-be director, choose to stand on, one thing is abundantly clear.

> **Straight Talk: You had better know why you are standing where you are and be prepared to explain your position to shareholders and, quite possibly, the media, other directors, and governance watchdogs, and potentially activist investors, too.**

If the organization on whose board you are serving has a combined CEO and board chair, you better be prepared to recite all the company has accomplished with that dynamic and how shareholders have benefited during that time. You need to know what those "wins" have been and how your vaunted leader helped produce them.

Likewise, if your enterprise has separated what are arguably its two most visible roles, you must be prepared to discuss why they are separated, when they were separated, and again, the performance that has ensued and what it means for a variety of stakeholders, including shareholders.

What matters most is performance, the pursuit of a sound strategy, having the right leaders in the right role, and driving consistent return on investment for shareholders.

Some companies, like those in our earlier example, have made so compelling a case on their sheer performance over time as to really mute this particular issue, which for the majority of American and multinational companies is a pressing priority on which they will face more pressure for change.

Yes, if it ain't broke, don't fix it. But as a director, you must regularly ask yourself and other directors whether the alignment or separation of the CEO and board chair roles is enabling growth and sustainability or actually holding your enterprise back.

Particularly if your board is going for growth or pursuing a new strategic agenda, you have to be prepared to make yourself heard and let nothing—including the current operating structure of your board and its bylaws—stand in your way.

Remember, planning for the eventual and even the potentially crisis-driven near-term succession of even the most accomplished and entrenched leader of your board and/or senior management team is your primary responsibility as a director. You owe it to yourself and to your shareholding constituents to make that a board priority, no matter whether anyone on the board challenges you. Even the emperor.

Chapter 7

Getting CEO Search and Succession Right the First Time: Don't Fumble the Handoff

What matters most when you are trying to find a new leader for your organization?

Over the course of our careers on corporate, university, and not-for-profit boards and advisory boards, attracting the best talent and effectively planning and orchestrating a smooth CEO succession process have been right at the top of the priorities list.

That was true years ago, and it remains true today for board directors and senior management leaders alike.

Successful organizations start with talented people (from "home-grown" high performers to top-notch leaders recruited externally), and they grow and prosper because of capable, confident, and sometimes courageous executive leadership. Their leaders understand that chainsaws are for cutting trees, not personnel.

The best employers in any industry buy *and* build great teams. They create a winning culture that winners want to join. They give people great opportunities to learn and grow and become leaders. In turn, the best people attract other high performers, and success builds on success.

Talent is your organization's most pivotal performance multiplier.

Your biggest nominating responsibility as a director is to ensure you have an inspiring, example-setting CEO who fits with your culture and strategic objectives and who will not embarrass the organization or disappoint stakeholders. Your next-biggest nominating task is to ensure you have a clear succession plan just as soon as you have named your

CEO, or at the very least, as soon as you have figured out that he or she is, in your mind, a "keeper."

THE TRUTH ABOUT TALENT

The best boards and directors constantly have their eye on talent. Discussions about talent, leadership, and organizational capabilities are built into their cultures and their board meeting agendas, either formally or informally.

These boards and directors are continually analyzing and assessing the performance of their CEO and they are mindful of how the industry environment, the competition, and internal priorities should shape the requirements for the next CEO. You must do the same to make one of your own biggest contributions to good governance.

Ensuring, at the very least, that the organization has the proverbial "CEO hit by a runaway beer truck" succession plan is very much your responsibility. It should be a screen on whether you join a board in the first place. You should ask about the organization's plans for CEO succession—no matter how uncomfortable that may make you or anyone else feel about it. If all you are met with is a shrug of the shoulders by someone who would know if there is a plan for CEO succession, particularly in a crisis situation, you would be best served to run the other way. It is that big a deal.

Being ahead of the curve on CEO succession and being ready to respond to any crisis involving the CEO are among your highest callings as a member of the board. You might do everything else right as a director— fight to increase dividends to shareholders, restructure board committees to align with emerging needs, and/or ward off a hostile takeover or help prevent an intrusion by cyber-criminals—but if you get CEO succession wrong or are unprepared for disaster, your reputation as a director will be toast—and the enterprise will be irreparably harmed.

There is much debate today about the role of the outgoing CEO on the process of finding his or her successor. This debate centers on whether the CEO should take a leading role or simply contribute as the board deems appropriate. I am firmly in the latter camp. After all, it is the board's highest calling to ensure for a smooth CEO succession and transition process. But yes, the outgoing CEO can usually provide positive guidance for the incumbent.

The outgoing CEO has much of his or her legacy wrapped in perceptions about the kind of hands that will take the organization forward into the future. At the very least, the departing CEO should have a voice—but no more than any one member of the board—in framing the requirements for the role.

The outgoing CEO might even be afforded a chance to meet his or her successor to offer some guidance and encouragement as the new CEO takes over the reins, if both parties agree it would be productive. The incumbent can learn from the experience, no doubt, but must also be mindful to make his or her own decisions about the best way forward—especially as the new CEO "on-boards" into the role.

The best CEOs actually create their own succession plans—and multiply the board's options for succession—because that is in the best, long-term interest of sustaining the organization. Jack Welch has been fond of saying that great leaders are not intimidated by the prospect of being replaced some day.

These leaders create the deep "bench strength" their organizations need to deliver above-average sales and profit growth. They give their executive teams the responsibility and flexibility to tackle complex business challenges as well as visibility with the organization's board to help directors fulfill their oversight mandate.

By building a superior leadership team around them, today's CEOs contribute to effective succession for their own role.

PUT THE "WHAT" BEFORE THE "WHO"

All too often, boards and directors rush into judgments about "who" should be recruited or promoted into a key leadership position—most often the chief executive's chair—before they have really invested adequately in discovering the answer to this critical, two-part question:

"What's it really going to take to be successful in the role and how will we know that?"

Yes, many organizations get so stuck on the "who?" question that they never get to the "what?" Many never advance to meaningfully and methodically constructing the elements of high performance in the role, and as a result, their search for a successor to the CEO results in nothing more than a parade of big-name, often big-company CEOs who'll gladly leave their current organization if only you pay them a king's ransom.

This, in and of itself, often leads organizations down the wrong path because it's easy for directors—especially in the case of a crisis-borne CEO search and even the most proactive and methodical succession exercise—to become enamored with the brand name cachet of someone else's CEO or the company he or she leads.

Do not be romanced by the fast-talking CEO search consultant with a penchant for dropping names at the drop of a hat. Do not be romanced by the marketing and storytelling about potential CEO candidates who've delivered the goods elsewhere and who could do the same for your organization. Before you can believe any of the hype—and it is out there in the case of high-profile CEOs—you have got to do your own homework before the process spins its way out of control.

If you are not careful and methodical, before you know it, the compensation consultants come running in explaining what it's going to take to construct a compelling "top quartile" compensation package—and voilà, before you know it, you have lost control of the CEO succession process.

The fact of the matter is that the big-name candidate is often not the best person for the job, and the best person for the job is often not a big-name candidate.

Yet, far too many corporate leaders zealously charge head-on to replace a departed executive or to fill a new leadership role using whatever position description someone in Human Resources has conjured or a retained executive search firm has pulled from its files.

The headlong push to recruit a new chief executive officer far too often leads to the pursuit of somebody else's sitting CEO. This assumes that the skills required for success in one industry or company will automatically transfer to a new one, which they may not. It also precludes 99.99 percent of the population who have not yet reached the CEO's role from consideration, even if some among this group who might currently sit in a competitor's "C-suite" are actually best qualified to be your organization's CEO, given how the role will evolve in the next three to five years.

It is no wonder more women and minorities haven't reached the CEO's post. If only sitting CEOs are being considered by your board, don't be surprised when someone points out the glaring lack of diversity on your management team, or your board, for that matter.

START WITH A BLANK SLATE

Though it may be intimidating to some, it's quite often best to start the process of filling an important leadership role with a blank slate.

Otherwise, you run the risk of literally replicating some other organization's CEO search. That could result when someone on the board, the CEO, or perhaps even an executive search consultant offers an example of a job specification for one of their clients' recently completed CEO searches. Or, if you are not careful, the runners-up in that process might suddenly be introduced as your leading CEO candidates.

Rather than discussing whether a candidate must bring a master's degree or PhD to the role or debating the number of years of experience required, today's directors would be wise to center their attention on the outcomes any individual should deliver 6 or 12 months after taking the job.

What are the results we are after? What do we need to have seen from our next leader that would prove his or her capability and deserve our trust as a board? How will the competitive landscape shift in the next 12 months? In the next two to three years?

The kind of "blank-slate" approach I would endorse and you should seriously consider as a director ensures that you start with the end in mind. That is, you and your board peers envision what success looks like at some point in the future and the evidence you'd all point to as a marker of exceptional performance.

From there, it is all about putting the focus on the experience, skills, and interpersonal leadership style required to attain the desired results. It may well be that what you need to find in your next CEO is precisely what the outgoing CEO brought to the table.

Or, more often than not in today's business environment, you will find a widely divergent set of experiences and skills are needed—and that you would be well served to consider highly qualified leaders who have never been a CEO before but who would relish the chance to prove what they can do in that role.

Never underestimate someone with all the right stuff who just has not been given the chance to lead at the highest level before. Sometimes, that person's "fire in the belly" and contagious excitement and spirit is enough to move mountains.

The results have to be there, of course. But if I have learned anything over the years, it is that the right people do not just bring a serious work ethic to their jobs each day. They also bring the internal drive and determination we so often see in the world of sports.

WHY PASSION REALLY MATTERS

Rod Stewart has a song called "Passion" that is pretty explicit about the need to have it. In fact, in one part, he belts out, "Even the president needs passion!"

Our point about passion is simply this: When we are looking for someone to fill an important management role, we look for his or her passion for the job. Most successful people we know have a passion for what they do.

I still vividly recall, when I was chancellor of Texas Tech University, visiting with a member of the Tech police force, and to illustrate my point about successful people and the passion they bring to their work, I remember this officer came up to me during a basketball game and related the following.

"Chancellor, just wanted you to know I was making my rounds the other night and went to the United Spirit Arena [Tech's basketball facility]. It was around 3 o'clock in the morning. Coach Knight was in his office looking at game videos over and over of the next team we were going to play. Just thought you'd like to know."

Now whether you like legendary coach Bob Knight or not, he is one of the most successful collegiate men's basketball coaches in the history of the game. His success is no accident because he has a passion for what he does.

He also made his players go to class, raised millions in library donations, and had hugely successful seasons while he was at Texas Tech—which is a lot more than I can say for some of the nation's best-known basketball programs. Bob Knight has passion for what he does best—and that is precisely why we hired him.

The same was true of Mike Leach, the former Texas Tech head football coach who at the time of this writing was head coach of the Washington State University Cougars football team.

During my tenure as Texas Tech chancellor, we flew to Oklahoma and interviewed Mike at the airport in Oklahoma City. He was Bob Stoops's offensive coordinator for the Oklahoma Sooners at the time. While we interviewed Mike, all he seemed to be interested in was diagramming passing plays he would use if we selected him to coach our Texas Tech football team.

More recently, Mike made headlines for acknowledging that his head is so constantly devoted to the X's and O's of collegiate football that he will ask anyone around him—a fan, a janitor he might greet in the hall, or anyone else who watches the game—for their own insights on how to get the best from the talent on his team.[1]

Once in a while, Mike says, that person will hit upon something that can be improved, and which, for reasons related to his being too close to the scene, sometimes cannot be revealed without with the help of someone with a different view of the action. Mike calls it the benefit of a fresh set of eyes—which is the reason why new directors with the right perspective are always sought out to serve on corporate, not-for-profit, institutional, and civic boards and advisory committees.

Mike was so passionate about the game and reinforced our view that he was such an offense-minded coach and tactical genius that we hired him that very day. I was impressed with Mike's passion for the game as I had been with Bob Knight's. It was clear that both men loved the games to which they have dedicated themselves more than their respective salaries.

LOOK 'EM IN THE EYE

I might not have figured out Bob Knight and Mike Leach were the best hires for these jobs had I not been personally involved in their recruitment. Given the pressures involved in my job then, and so many competing demands for my time, it would have been very easy to delegate the job of recruiting our men's head basketball and football coaches.

It has been said that fatherhood is 90 percent just showing up and being there. For our part, as it should be with today's directors, recruiting new leaders into the organization—especially a new chief executive officer—should be job number one.

You need to be involved. At the very least you need to be consulted and know how the process is unfolding and who the key actors are.

But for the very best impact (and the soundest nights' sleep), you need to be personally engaged with candidates, much in the same way Texas's own Michael Dell has been linked to the recruitment of key executives over the years.

You can imagine how many high-performing leaders from a variety of technology companies were impressed over the years and ultimately moved to join Dell after Michael himself would get on the phone, give the candidate a call, and tell him or her why he wanted them to join the Dell leadership team.

Our point is that you have got to make it personal, whether you are recruiting from the outside or promoting from the inside. In fact, any CEO candidate worth his or her salt would want to meet you whether you initiate that opportunity or not.

Whether or not you are on the board's Nominating Committee, as a director you have a right—a duty, really—to stay close to the process, to provide timely and relevant inputs based on your own experience, and to keep your fellow board members and their agents accountable for the process. Better yet, be directly involved in the process and lead it from start to finish—from the "blank slate" I campaigned for earlier, all the way to toasting the arrival of a new chief executive.

Particularly in the case of recruiting a new CEO from the outside, as a director you owe it to your shareholders to get to know the candidates, ask tough questions, and look each one squarely in the eye to try to read their motivations—regardless of what they might tell you. Of course, a thorough background check will help pick up anything you might have missed or been misled about.

After all, any qualified CEO candidate would rank as an outstanding interviewer—maybe even a capable bullshitter. Some of the most charismatic, charming CEO candidates might lead you down the garden path. It has happened before, and to some otherwise capable boards and directors.

But what really counts is what CEO candidates are willing to invest to deliver the results you need—and whether that mission syncs with their passion. Passionate leaders will work a lot harder and longer than anyone else because they care so deeply about what they are doing. Failure is not an option.

One of the best ways to get to the bottom of a CEO candidate's intentions and drive is to catch them outside the office—and outside their custom-tailored suit. That is why, as a director, particularly as a Nominating Committee chair or member, you would be well served to try to engage with the candidate on a Saturday, at their home, perhaps even between family commitments such as a Little League game, soccer tournament, or birthday party for their child or grandchild.

In our combined experience, connecting with leaders on a more personal, one-to-one level is best accomplished away from the office and certainly outside the boardroom. This is where you can get to the important straight talk about what they want to achieve in their life, what they have left to prove, and to whom.

We can think of lots of people we have interviewed over the years who were highly qualified on paper, but a lousy conversationalist. Who brought impeccable credentials, but who lacked common sense. People who interviewed beyond compare, only to disappoint with how they tipped a good waiter, how they spoke down to a hotel concierge, or otherwise revealed real personal insecurities and character flaws by belittling others.

You see, we are not only concerned with how someone acts Monday through Friday in the work environment. If this person you're interviewing is a potential leader of your enterprise, you better know how they spend their off-hours. You need to know how they conduct themselves away from work and the kind of legacy and reputation they're building in their own community.

You have got to see what they look like in a pair of jeans. No, we are not referring in any way to their physical shape, but rather, their sense of comfort in their own skin, when their typical corporate guard is not up, and in the company of people who are not their subordinates. Ideally, we want to see them carry themselves with the confidence and composure they would espouse in a suit, and we want to know they have a sense of humility and human decency packed right along with them.

As a director, this more casual, less scripted view of the candidate may be incredibly revealing. We want the leader who demonstrates the utmost consistency between their "CEO persona" and their neighborhood or community persona. We want the person who is not afraid of or above rolling up their sleeves to get an important job done, or to help in a moment of real challenge or peril for someone else.

We want to look the CEO candidate squarely in the eye and feel in their reflection a sense of confidence that we know the person, we know what motivates him or her, and we have a pretty good sense for why people see him or her as a leader—in the finest suit or in their Saturday street clothes.

There are lots of good reasons you should look 'em in the eye before you hire anyone, let alone a new CEO or executive-level leader on whose shoulders your entire organization's future will in some measure rest.

Consider the case we heard about just recently from a friend who was interviewing a candidate who looked particularly good on paper.

During the video interview, however, this particular management candidate kept looking to his left, time and again, rather than toward the camera and in the direction of the interviewer. It soon became clear that the individual was actually taking cues on how to answer each question from an executive coach sitting comfortably and conveniently outside of the range of the camera. Suffice to say that candidate did not get the job.

As a candidate, you simply cannot mail it in. If you don't have the chops to withstand a tough, probing, and perhaps somewhat unnerving interview, you probably would not last long in the face of the escalating pressure facing corporate leaders today.

And as an employer, you certainly should not make a critical hiring decision over the phone via videoconference or based solely on someone's word. You have to look 'em in the eye, shake the person's hand, and commit to relating to that individual on a human level.

YOUR SUCCESSION CHECKLIST

As a director, you have to put CEO succession and the organization's talent agenda—from hiring and firing to promotions and retention—on your short-list of top governance priorities. You always have to be ready to confidently answer these questions not only to your satisfaction, but to shareholders' satisfaction first and foremost:

1. Are we ready to orchestrate the CEO succession process?

2. Are we learning about the requirements for our next CEO even while our current CEO is comfortable in the lead?

3. Are we willing to gather all the intelligence we can about what we need in our next CEO while at the same time remain willing to start with a blank slate?

4. Do we have a crisis-borne CEO succession plan in place that would cover us at least temporarily if our current CEO gets hit by the proverbial bus or runaway beer truck?

5. Are we seeing more than just the CEO at board meetings? If not, why not?

6. Are we engaging with the CEO's "C-suite" in a manner that would give us as a board the necessary insights to determine who among them might rank as potential successors to the sitting CEO?

7. Are we as directors really getting to know our CEO candidates? Are we seeing them in their Saturday blue jeans? Or are we basing our judgments about them based purely on what someone else (like our chosen search consultant) is telling us about these folks? Are we looking 'em in the eye?

8. How are we soliciting candidate referrals from the board? How are we se- lecting our search consultant and what do we know about their process and the actual business results delivered by the CEOs they have recruited for other organizations?

9. Are we talking about CEO compensation—and reasonable limits on that compensation—before we get pushed to the brink by a sought-after CEO candidate?

10. Have we generated a consensus in terms of the business results the next CEO has to deliver? Have we agreed on a performance measurement plan against which to assess our new CEO and his or her compensation package?

As you consider these critical issues for the organization on whose board you serve, think of these as opportunities to develop the right process and to attract the very best leaders to the enterprise.

If you are too insulated from its talent agenda, you could be facing an elevated risk of being surprised or unprepared to face a crisis situation. If you do not have the visibility you need to see how people are being brought into the organization, you need to get it. It is up to you. No one else will volunteer the wins and losses that pile up every day, be they counted in candidates who took a pass on your team and went elsewhere or the employees who were overlooked for promotion for the umpteenth time.

As a director, you wield incredible influence, both formal and informal, both professional and personal. If you take that responsibility seriously, you will surely invest time discovering your organization's technology and its strategy. But its biggest competitive resource is its people—so you've got to get to the bottom of why they're coming and why they're going.

As an investor in any company, you have got to look at the income that is coming in and the expenses that are eating it up. So, too, must you understand the flow of talent into and out of the organization on whose board or advisory board you serve.

Only then can you get a full and accurate view of what your organization—and its leaders—are truly capable of achieving for the shareholders and other parties who are counting on all of you.

Chapter 8

The Audit Committee: The Board's "Fire Department"

With the passage of the Sarbanes-Oxley Act by Congress in 2002 coupled with events impacting shareholders, employee pensions, financial markets, and the public in general over the last several years, Audit Committees of American corporations now play perhaps the most active role in corporate oversight.

This increased responsibility for oversight by the Audit Committee includes the integrity of the company's financial statements, independent auditors, internal auditors, internal financial controls, risk management, and legal and regulatory compliance together with many other responsibilities.

ORGANIZATION AND QUALIFICATIONS OF THE AUDIT COMMITTEE

Pursuant to federal law, the listing standards of the New York Stock Exchange (NYSE), and the NASDAQ Stock Market (NASDAQ), every publicly traded company in the United States is required to have an Audit Committee of at least *three* members. Regardless of its size, it must be composed *entirely* (emphasis added) of independent directors who meet the "independence" requirements outlined in SOX Section 301 and the Exchange Act Rule 10A–3(6)(1).[1]

Additionally, SEC Regulation S-K requires that a company disclose in its annual report whether or not the committee includes at least one "financial expert," and if not, why not.[2]

The Audit Committee is also directly responsible for appointing, compensating, and terminating the company's independent auditors, which requires rotation "off" every five years.[3]

A comprehensive written charter is required for the Audit Committee that must set forth the committee's duties and responsibilities as well as required areas of oversight of the committee.[4]

Federal law and NYSE and NASDAQ Rules have become very detailed and complex relating to the organization and responsibilities of the Audit Committee. The discussion that follows will examine the key areas of responsibility and oversight.

Audit Committee members must be competent in financial matters, active, and engaged. If not, ask them to step down. It is the board's busiest committee. If it's not, it should be. It has been referred to as "the board's fire department," specifically having duties for "anything related to risk."[5]

AUDIT COMMITTEE CHARTER

Straight Talk: In order for an Audit Committee to be effective, particularly with increased responsibilities, it must have a comprehensive charter in place that covers the full range of the committee's responsibilities.

A well-written charter for the Audit Committee is like a constitution for a country. It outlines and delineates the many responsibilities of the committee and gives guidance on how to carry out these responsibilities. The first order of business for the committee chair is to make sure the other members of the committee are familiar with the charter. It is a necessary backstop to make sure the committee covers the full range of its responsibilities under Sarbanes-Oxley as well as SEC requirements. It should be periodically reviewed and updated. If your company's Audit Committee Charter is catching dust, this would be a good time to review it. For instance, has it been updated to incorporate the auditing and oversight of your company's information technology procedures and systems? Unless your company has a special board committee to oversee information technology or IT as it is appropriately called, it is likely that such oversight falls to the Audit Committee, particularly as it relates to financial matters, internal controls, and risk management.

For NYSE and NASDAQ listed companies, the Audit Committee Charter must include committee duties and responsibilities required by Rule 10A-3 of the Exchange Act. These include:

1. Appointing, compensating, and retaining a public accounting firm and overseeing the firm's work in preparing and issuing the audit report
2. Establishing procedures for processing employee complaints on internal accounting controls or audit matters as well as anonymous complaints regarding questionable accounting
3. Having the authority to engage independent counsel and other advisers necessary to carry out its duties
4. Having appropriate funding to pay the independent auditors, advisers, and administrative costs.[6]

There are some variations in the requirements for Audit Committee Charters between companies listed on NYSE and those listed on NASDAQ, provided that both are required to address responsibilities under Rule 10A-3 of the Exchange Act as listed above.

For NYSE listed companies, the Audit Committee Charter must include assisting board oversight of the integrity of the company's financial statements, compliance with legal and regulatory requirements, independent auditor qualification and independence, performance of the company's internal audit functions and independent auditors, and preparing the disclosure required by Regulation S-K Item 407 (d)(3)(i) relating to the Audit Committee report included in the annual proxy statement.[7]

Additional NYSE Rules require:

1. Reviewing the independent auditor's annual report describing:
    a. Internal quality controls procedures
    b. Material issues raised by the internal quality control review, peer review, or government inquiry or investigation within the last five years
    c. All relationships between the independent auditor and the company to assess the firm's independence
2. Meeting with management to discuss annual and quarterly audited financial statements, including review of "Management's Discussion and Analysis of Financial Condition and Results of Operations" (MD&A)
3. Discussing earnings press releases and financial information and earnings guidance given
4. Discussing policies with respect to risk assessment and risk management
5. Meeting separately from time to time with management and with internal and independent auditors

6. Reviewing with the independent auditor any audit problems and management's response

7. Setting clear hiring policies for employees or former employees of the independent auditor

8. Reporting regularly to the board of directors

9. Annually evaluating the Audit Committee[8]

For NASDAQ listed companies, the charter must specify (1) the scope and how it carries out responsibilities including structure, process, and membership requirements, (2) responsibilities for receipt from outside auditors of a written statement delineating relationships between auditors and the company and responsibility for a dialogue with auditors on relationships that might impact auditor independence and objectivity, and for taking or recommending that the full board take action to oversee outside auditor independence, and (3) the committee's purpose of overseeing the company's accounting and financial reporting processes and financial statement audits.[9]

Lastly, whether NYSE or NASDAQ, SEC Regulation S-K requires that the company's proxy statement disclose whether the current Audit Committee Charter is available on the company's website, and if so, the website address.[10]

> **Straight Talk: Unless your company has a special committee designated to handle information technology and cybersecurity oversight, it will fall under the Audit Committee's responsibilities.**

In short, the Audit Committee Charter is the repository and guidepost for all the committee's legal and regulatory responsibilities. Use it as your backstop to ensure compliance and facilitate transparency and completeness in your financial reporting responsibilities. Use it in formulating your checklists for full compliance. Keep it current and review it periodically for needed amendments to meet the demands of a changing, fast-paced reporting environment.

There are a number of sample Audit Committee Charters online that are easily accessed. The Institute of Internal Auditors' "Model Audit Committee Charter" is a good starting point. Most likely, you will need to tailor the charter to meet the requirements of your own business enterprise because one size does not necessarily fit all. Just be sure you review it with both your internal and external auditors as well as legal counsel, management, and other board members to be sure you have included all of your many legal and regulatory responsibilities.

In the final analysis, the Audit Committee Charter is your Audit Committee's written constitution. Use it and follow it as such.

INDEPENDENT FINANCIAL EXPERT

Straight Talk: There must be at least one member of the committee who is classified as a "financial expert" as that term is defined in the SEC's rules promulgated under 407 of the Sarbanes-Oxley Act of 2002. However, you do not have to be a CPA to be considered a financial expert.

The act in Section 407 and SEC Regulation S-K requires that public companies disclose in filings whether or not their Audit Committee includes at least one "financial expert" who must be named and determined to be independent of management.

It is important to note that under SEC rules, to qualify as a "financial expert" that individual must have each of the following qualifications:

1. An understanding of generally accepted accounting principles (GAAP) and financial statements
2. The ability to use such principles in connection with assessments of estimates, accruals, and reserves
3. Experience and knowledge of financial statements to a level of complexity raised by the company's other financials or at least having supervised such a person with such knowledge
4. An understanding of internal controls for financials
5. An understanding of how the audit committee works[11]

The rules further provide that these attributes *must* have been acquired in at least one of the following ways:

1. Education and experience as a principal financial officer, accounting officer, controller, public accountant, or auditor
2. Experience overseeing or assessing the performance of companies or public accountants preparing, evaluating, or auditing financial statements
3. Other relevant experience[12]

It is also important to note that having previously served on an Audit Committee does not by itself qualify one as a financial expert. Even having served as an accountant, auditor, CFO, or controller doesn't automatically qualify one as a financial expert.

Likewise, before an individual can be designated as a financial expert, he or she must embody the highest personal and professional integrity, which means that anyone with a prior disciplinary action will be suspect.

In short, the board should thoroughly consider all relevant facts in a person's history and background before designating a financial expert.

THE AUDIT COMMITTEE AND THE INDEPENDENT AUDITOR

Straight Talk: Hiring, paying, and terminating the independent auditors are the responsibility of the Audit Committee, not management.

It is obvious that an independent auditor must be a person or firm that examines a company's records and transactions with which he/she/it is not affiliated. Sarbanes-Oxley made it clear that (1) the Audit Committee, not management, hires the outside independent auditor and that (2) the entire Audit Committee is made up of independent directors.[13]

This change has imposed significant responsibilities on the committee and must be taken seriously. In working with the independent auditors, it is also a requirement that those designated to perform the independent audits are limited to five-year terms and must be rotated off this assignment after their term expires.

The relationship with the committee also extends to the independent auditors' compensation, which the Audit Committee, not management, determines.

Thus, the relationship between the independent auditors and the committee is important. It is a relationship that cannot be "cozy" or "patronizing" but should be anchored on mutual respect.

The goal should be one of fostering candor, transparency, and integrity in all aspects of the examination.

As an Audit Committee member, one might consider the following guidance in dealing with the company's independent auditors:

1. Make sure the individual or firm is competent and qualified to conduct the audits.

2. Make sure they are independent of the company in all respects, being cautious about any personal or long-standing relationships with management. It is a good idea to have the legal staff or outside counsel make sure they are in fact independent.

3. Make sure the compensation paid is "reasonable and necessary" for the plan of work and work completed. The committee should be vigilant about audit expenses.

4. Have periodic meetings to be advised of developments and findings as the audits are ongoing. It is better to get a "jump," as the saying goes, on bad news before you read about it in the news.

5. Make periodic inquiries about how the independent and internal auditors are effectively working together to ensure transparency and accurate financial reporting.

Another requirement is that the Audit Committee must meet in executive session, without management, to ensure there is a forum where both the independent and internal auditors can speak candidly with the committee without fear of retribution.[14]

In addressing the independent auditor, the committee should develop an open dialogue about all aspects of internal financial controls and risk management.

At the end of this chapter you will find a full range of suggested questions for the independent auditors at Audit Committee meetings and in executive session. Over time, each Audit Committee should develop its own set of boilerplate questions tailored to the particular business that the company conducts, to make sure all aspects of the committee's and board's financial responsibilities are inquired about.

The importance of an effective and credible independent auditor firm cannot be overstated. It can make or break a company. It monitors the pulse of a company's financial performance, and when done right, raises flags that result in timely remedial actions before financial issues become catastrophic.

THE AUDIT COMMITTEE AND THE INTERNAL AUDITOR

Most public companies have both internal and independent or external auditors to adequately provide credible financials.

There are several differences between the two, the most significant being that public companies are not required to have internal auditors but are mandated under Sarbanes-Oxley to have independent external auditors.

The other big difference is that internal auditors are "in house" and full time on the premises, and they report to the Audit Committee for oversight.[15]

> **Straight Talk: An effective internal audit staff should monitor day-to-day financial risks and internal controls, and be a fraud detection police force.**

It is imperative that the Audit Committee, in order to perform its required functions, have a strong dialogue with the internal auditors and staff. It is also essential that the internal and independent auditors work together to ensure oversight of internal controls, financial risk management, and credible financial reporting.

No matter how efficiently a company performs, you will always need to be vigilant for fraud and theft. It just happens, frequently by individuals who think they can game the system. Internal auditors should pursue fraud, waste, and theft allegations with a vengeance and develop a reputation for having "no tolerance" for such occurrences.

Any corporate financial transaction should be fair game for internal auditors as well as external auditors. This includes management's expense accounts. Through the years, internal auditors can be an extremely effective deterrent for corporate financial misconduct.

Employees are generally more forthcoming about problems to "in-house" auditors. They are onsite 24/7 and as such, depending on staff size, can develop specialized areas such as IT and cybersecurity, which are needed these days in corporate America.

Some major companies have gone entirely to outside independent auditors as a cost-saving measure. However, this is a decision that merits considerable thought. In most companies, they will more than offset their costs.

THE AUDIT COMMITTEE AND THE CFO

A special and candid working relationship founded on mutual respect is necessary between the chief financial officer and the Audit Committee chair.

They should visit regularly between board meetings. This is necessary since the quarterly earnings press release must first be reviewed for content and accuracy, and approved by the chair of the Audit Committee before it goes public at the "earnings call" by management.[16]

The same holds true of the quarterly earnings report to the SEC, the 10-Q and also the 10-K—the annual report, which must be reviewed and approved by the full Audit Committee before release.[17]

Normally, this is done by a scheduled conference call with the Audit Committee, management, the independent and internal auditors, all in on the call to review and verify the information for the committee's questions and review.

> **Straight Talk: Make sure management has distributed "confidential" drafts of the press release, 10-Qs, and 10-Ks to the Audit Committee prior to the review date and Audit Committee meeting, with sufficient time to review the material.**

Needless to say, these periodic meetings of the Audit Committee require that its members be willing to give more of their time than members on perhaps any other committee.

Because of complexities in the law and regulatory mandates, the CFO is the essential bridge between corporate finances and Audit Committee oversight.

A strong working relationship between the Audit Committee and the CFO helps anticipate financial issues, and timely communication avoids unpleasant surprises. Periodic meetings between the CFO and the Audit Committee chair are not only desirable but contribute to an organization's financial affairs running smoothly.

Audit Committees also expect the CFO to have the CEO's ear to align financial strategies for growth and profitability.

Regular meetings and briefings not only help develop good lines of communication, but the exposure to staff helps the committee gain confidence in the finance organization's personnel.

Audit Committees appreciate a CFO who has insight in forecasting and budgeting, and who takes a leading role in managing enterprise risks.

MONITORING INTERNAL CONTROLS AND FINANCIAL RISK MANAGEMENT

Conceptually, if one gets to the fundamental theory of Sarbanes-Oxley, it was in reality a well-intentioned post-Enron piece of federal legislation designed to protect shareholder investments and employees' pension plans from fraudulent acts and significant financial misstatements.

The resulting costs, just for accounting expenses, have been astronomical for public companies. Two accounting principles override in the operation of public companies—management of financial risks and candor in reporting earnings. Section 404 of Sarbanes-Oxley *requires* management to certify that the company's internal control procedures are adequate and effective.[18]

This requirement manifests itself primarily in two ways: (1) internal financial controls and (2) financial risk management.

What internal controls must be put in place to monitor financial risks?

Internal controls can be defined as methods for measuring an organization's operational objectives and efficiencies that provide reasonable assurance of the achievement of reliable financial information, all while in compliance with applicable laws and regulations.[19]

Effective internal controls are an early detection system for financial risks. They are crucial barometers that sound alarm bells to auditors, management, and ultimately directors so that a timely resolution of critical issues can be managed.

Examples include performance evaluations, budgets, operating ratios, prior year (YOY) and month comparisons, return on investments, market share, same-store comparisons, and a balance sheet's cash flow and profit and loss statements. In short, internal controls are a timely measurement of a company's financial performance. Oversight and monitoring of internal controls and risk management are key responsibilities of the Audit Committee.

ENTER PCAOB—THE PUBLIC COMPANY ACCOUNTING OVERSIGHT BOARD

Straight Talk: The Audit Committee and full board, when practicable, should have periodic updates of the PCAOB rules by the financial officers of the company.

With the passage of Sarbanes-Oxley in 2002, this board was created as a privately run for-profit corporation to oversee the audits and accounting standards for public companies.[20]

What Audit Committees must focus on through internal controls is the occurrence of deficiencies. A host of terms have been defined by PCAOB, and it is confusing to determine what each is meant to identify.

Consider these terms that arise in analyzing internal controls and financial risk management:

Deficiency

Significant deficiency

Internal control deficiency

Material weakness

Restatement

A "restatement," meaning a revision of one or more of a company's financial statements previously issued and found to be in error, should be necessary when calculation mistakes or fraudulent accounting activity is discovered. Not all restatements are the same.[21]

It may or may not be "material." A deficiency exists when an internal financial control does not exist or does not detect the control objective it is designed to detect.[22]

A "significant deficiency" is a deficiency in internal controls that is less severe than a "material weakness" yet important enough to merit the attention of those in charge of oversight.[23]

A "deficiency" is a missing, defectively designed, or poorly operated internal control over financial reporting. A material weakness is one or more deficiencies in internal controls for financial reporting such that there is a reasonable probability that a material misstatement of the company's financial statements will not be prevented or detected in a timely manner.

In determining whether deficiencies are material weaknesses, the Audit Committee should review paragraphs 62–70 of PCAOB Auditing Standards No. 5.[24]

The independent auditors' required communications to the committee, the board, and management should distinguish between those matters considered significant deficiencies and those considered material weaknesses.

A restatement of a previous financial statement is necessary when it is determined that the previous financial statement contains a material inaccuracy that is severe enough to require a restatement.[25]

The reason a finding of materiality is important is to determine whether a restatement is necessary. A restatement is a major undertaking, but your shareholders deserve to know if you've made a major financial mistake or oversight that impacts the bottom line. Since your CEO and CFO are required to certify that the 10-Q and 10-K filings are accurate and the Audit Committee has to certify the audit, serious consequences can ensue if you don't detect errors, correct them, and report them publicly if they are a material weakness or serious factual error.

THE AUDIT COMMITTEE'S ROLE IN FILING AN 8-K AMENDMENT

> **Straight Talk: A material change in the financial condition or operations of a company requires filing a Form 8-K Amendment with the SEC.**

Section 409 of the Sarbanes-Oxley Act, specifically Section 13(1), which amended the Exchange Act, requires public companies to promptly disclose any additional information that reflects material changes in the financial condition or operations of a company for the protection of investors and the public. This is generally the case if the company became aware of such additional information after the expiration of more than 48 hours of a filing. Thus, for example, if a CEO resigns or there is a misleading or inaccurate statement in a prior filing of a 10-Q or 10-K that amounts to a material misstatement, Form 8-K must be publicly filed with the SEC to notify investors and the public about such events.[26]

> **Straight Talk: Always get the concurrence of your independent auditors to determine if an error is material and requires a restatement. A rough guideline on materiality is a mistake or inaccuracy that impacts 5 percent or more of continuing operations.[27]**

THE AUDIT COMMITTEE AS A "CATCH-ALL"

> **Straight Talk: Some companies have a tendency to "hand off" any internal issue relating to oversight, even if outside the committee's traditional purview, to the Audit Committee.**

A word of caution here because this practice is fairly common, with management and directors wanting to be overly cautious these days. The point is that the Audit Committee must first and foremost be focused on *financial controls and risk management*. That is and should be its primary charge and focus. When other issues arise concerning internal oversight that do not pertain to financial risks, should the Audit Committee undertake oversight and propose solutions?

The answer is complicated since all committees must be vigilant about corporate performance, and many would argue that just about any issue affecting internal and external corporate performance impacts the bottom line and therefore is part of financial risk management. This is an important discussion because the chair of the Audit Committee must ensure that the committee has the resources to stay focused on its primary role: assessing financial risks.

Suppose, for example, an issue arises concerning employee safety that escalates to board levels. Should this be the job of the Audit Committee to oversee?

Certainly this issue could affect finances—but which committee should do the oversight? In terms of guidance, the committee cannot become the company's "junk drawer" for any issue requiring oversight. It is there that the committee chair has the responsibility to be the gatekeeper in order to keep the committee focused on internal controls and financial risk management. That being said, a conscientious chair will make sure the problem requiring board oversight is handled and does not "fall through the cracks," as the expression goes. The worst thing you can do is to ignore a problem. It may be necessary to empower a special committee to handle the problem. However, a conscientious board will understand, and by working with management will get the problem resolved—just don't neglect it simply because you're focused on financial risk management.

THE AUDIT COMMITTEE'S ROLE IN FILING THE 10-Q AND THE 10-K

The 10-Q and the 10-K coupled with the annual Proxy Statement are the heart and soul documents of a company's financial transparency.

We previously discussed these mandatory filings with the SEC in chapters 2 and 3.

The Audit Committee has to approve these filings before they are submitted to the full board and then to the SEC, so it becomes increasingly important to understand their content. Essentially, they are a public disclosure of a company's financials so that shareholders, investors, lenders, and regulatory agencies can make intelligent assessments about the company's financial condition. They impact sales, acquisitions, and a variety of financial activities.

Also, since the Audit Committee has to recommend the annual independent audit to the board for inclusion in the 10-K, it is essential that the committee read these filings and compare them with prior filings, and have an understanding of what is being reported and what has changed.[28]

Likewise, the CEO and CFO must certify the truthfulness and the accuracy of the filings.[29]

In short, as an Audit Committee member, before signing off on a 10-Q (quarterly) and especially a 10-K (annual) report, be sure to:

1. Read it carefully for mistakes.
2. Read the highlighted provisions that have changed from your last filing (at least have management highlight the changes).
3. Review any concerns and raise questions with both your internal and independent auditors.
4. Review it carefully with management.
5. Make sure the full Audit Committee and the board review the 10-K.
6. Carefully examine the "forward looking" statements.
7. Ask legal counsel for comments.

All of these steps certainly reinforce your fiduciary responsibilities under Sarbanes-Oxley and to your shareholders.

It is a good practice to invite the full board to the Audit Committee sessions reviewing the 10-Qs and the 10-K.

THE AUDIT COMMITTEE AND THE CODE OF ETHICS

Just as an Audit Committee must have financial experts, the company must also (under 406 of Sarbanes-Oxley) disclose annually whether or not it has adopted a Code of Ethics for the company's principal officers.[30]

This Code of Ethics must conform to certain minimum standards including honest and ethical conduct, dealing with conflicts of interest, fair and accurate disclosures in reports, compliance with laws and regulations, and prompt reporting procedures for violations.

The Code of Ethics must be made available to the public, and any changes to the code need to be addressed in amended public filings. Although ethical conduct is a companywide responsibility, since it is an integral part of Sarbanes-Oxley's dictates, the Audit Committee should monitor full compliance.[31]

ADDITIONAL ISSUES THAT MAY COME BEFORE AUDIT COMMITTEES

As a member of the Audit Committee you will be asked from time to time to deal with issues that come up that are distracting, time consuming, and downright unpleasant. Unpleasant situations arising in business are inevitable. You might as well be equipped to handle them, since most likely they will originate or be referred to the Audit Committee. Some of these include:

1. Anonymous and nonanonymous complaints on a variety of subjects, including whistle-blower complaints
2. Shareholder derivative lawsuits
3. Regulation FD issues relating to selective disclosures
4. Patent troll lawsuits
5. Insider trading issues
6. Management expense audits
7. "Off-balance-sheet" transactions
8. Fraud and major defalcations
9. Foreign Corrupt Practices Act (FCPA) infractions

> **Straight Talk: The Audit Committee must, under federal law, establish procedures for handling whistle-blower, anonymous, and nonanonymous complaints.**

As an Audit Committee member you cannot let your personal opinions and feelings override your obligations to address these issues as they arise. There is a natural distrust of whistle-blowers and anonymous complaints. That being said, Audit Committees are required by law to establish procedures for accepting employee complaints, both anonymously and nonanonymously, that concern questionable accounting or auditing matters, as well as anonymous complaints concerning financial matters. Thus one of your responsibilities, as a member of the Audit Committee, is to make sure there are established procedures in Audit Committee charters to process and resolve such complaints.[32]

When you review such a complaint you need to have procedures in place that govern your handling of them responsively to conclusion and recommend action if the complaints are credible.

> **Straight Talk: In exceptional circumstances, it may become necessary for the Audit Committee to seek outside legal counsel for advice.**

On rare occasions it may become necessary for the committee to engage outside and independent legal counsel for advice. The Audit Committee is authorized to act in its individual capacity in so doing. Obtaining outside independent counsel can be time consuming and expensive so this practice should be used sparingly. For example, if an intentional misstatement is discovered in financials that implicates management, it might become necessary to engage outside counsel to advise the committee as you investigate the facts and prepare to file your 8-K Amendment.[33]

Some of these actions, like patent troll lawsuits and shareholder derivative actions, are usually nothing but corporate "shakedowns" for attorney fees.

Patent trolls continuously police patents, particularly for software, for any possible infringements. The problem becomes chronic when patent infringement actions relate to software content.

Frankly, the patent system has not adapted well to the ever-changing information technology world. At times, instead of encouraging innovation, the current process seems to discourage it, particularly when it comes to software. A clever lawyer can allege that almost any piece of corporate software is related to some prior patent. The problem occurs with the costs of litigation. Companies have to respond to these lawsuits, conduct expensive discovery proceedings that heavily favor the plaintiff, and legal costs skyrocket. Many companies will settle these lawsuits simply because it is cheaper to settle than to undertake prolonged litigation. Congress should enact legislation to protect patents but encourage innovation, particularly when it comes to software development. A more balanced procedure for handling discovery and frivolous lawsuits should be enacted.

Another area ripe for corporate "shakedowns" is in shareholder derivative suits. In these cases, corporations in effect are asked to sue themselves to take corrective action for some act or omission that is alleged to have resulted in damages to shareholders.

In reality what happens is that pension funds and other investors will buy a small block of stock and then when an event occurs will engage legal counsel to file shareholder derivative actions. In many cases, all that is sought is a shakedown for attorney fees. Amazingly, cases exist in which lawyers have actually admitted this.

Again, this is another area where Congress or state legislatures should enact major reforms.

> **Straight Talk: If your company is sued in one of these types of actions, make sure legal checks your comprehensive general liability insurance or other policies that might provide coverage.**

Another unpleasant incident will occur when management expense accounts are questioned. It seems that no matter how generous a corporation is in its compensation of officers and employees, improper charges and activities will occur.

It is utterly amazing what items sometimes appear on expense accounts. Lavish dinners, expensive liquor bills, strip clubs, gentlemen's clubs, and ladies' clubs are not ordinarily in the purview of supervised conduct by a corporation. However, they can become the business of the Audit Committee if they appear on a corporate credit card and expense accounts. Sometimes employees get carried away with corporate credit cards, so it is incumbent on the Audit Committee to give them friendly reminders that such conduct is being monitored.

The leaders of major American and global corporations have seen their careers unravel and their companies' brands and shareholder relations damaged because of indiscretions and outrageous, stupid lapses in judgment related to corporate expense accounts. We simply could not make some of this stuff up!

This is an area where the internal auditor can be extremely effective. The Audit Committee should require that a review of management and employees' expenses should periodically be in the company's annual audit plan.

Any off-balance-sheet transactions should be flagged and carefully investigated by the Audit Committee. Off-balance-sheet transactions brought Enron down and were largely the genesis of Sarbanes-Oxley.

The solution to any off-balance-sheet transaction is simply this—disclose it in your filings and report it publicly in your 10-Qs and 10-K.

An example might be a transaction in a foreign country that is governed by different auditing standards. Simply disclose this in your filings. No off-balance-sheet transaction should be kept from your shareholders.

Lastly, you might be required to investigate an FCPA (Foreign Corrupt Practices Act) violation.

> **Straight Talk: The Audit Committee should ensure that your company has a process in place to educate management and employees about the Foreign Corrupt Practices Act (FCPA).**

This act was passed to ensure that American corporations maintain high ethical standards in international dealings. The practical effect is that American companies have to behave and not engage in acts that could be considered bribery under American legal standards. It has severe sanctions for violators. If your company has international business, get briefed on the FCPA.[34]

Also, all Audit Committee members should be aware of Regulation FD of the Securities and Exchange Commission (SEC).

This regulation, which was enacted in 2000 by the SEC, requires the public disclosure of material information to *all* investors at the same time in response to any selective disclosure.[35]

It generally comes into play when management, sometimes inadvertently, makes a disclosure to an analyst or investor that contains nonpublic information that could impact a stock trade or company operations. If such an allegation is made or discovered, the Audit Committee should immediately conduct an investigation. If the selective disclosure is determined to have occurred, then the disclosure must be made public by the public filing of an 8-K Amendment.

It is important to note that such selective disclosures can be made by family members and nonbusiness associates, and it can give rise to liability as a form of insider trading.

INSIDER TRADING

For decades, Congress has tried to pass laws providing for insider trading penalties where the release of nonpublic information by a corporate "insider" results in third parties profiteering with publicly traded stock. The Insider Trading Auctions Act of 1984 and the Insider Trading and Securities Exchange Act of 1988 provide for insider trading penalties of some three times the profits gained from the illicit trade.

Through the years the courts (and prosecutors) have expanded the reach of these laws, particularly to third-party "tips" that may influence illegal profiteering of publicly traded stock.

An "insider" includes by definition a company's officers, directors, or person in control of at least 10 percent of a company's stock. It is clear that when insiders use nonpublic information gained from their fiduciary capacity, a prosecution can occur for their fraudulent misconduct.[36]

A more difficult situation arises when these insiders tip or inform their friends who are not insiders. The individual who receives the tip, and may take unfair advantage on a stock transaction, is not by definition an insider.

Gradually, the courts have curtailed the extension of insider trading by overturning several convictions of traders because it could not be proven that each of the people participating in a chain of insider information actually benefited. Apparently this means that all the parties participating in an insider trade have to benefit from it or at least prove that the person receiving a tip knew that the person providing the nonpublic information would benefit from it.

Since the Supreme Court refused to review the appellate court's ruling, the requirement of knowledge of a benefit will likely remain the law. Many specialize in intelligence gathering on stock exchanges for clients trying to gather credible information about stock values and opportunities.

As a director you must remember that your first duty is your fiduciary responsibility to your shareholders. Any actions on your part trying to capitalize on nonpublic information about your company is bad business. It is easy to disclose nonpublic information—over coffee, at parties, at social events, and even in speeches. So, the prudent practice is to refrain from discussing any nonpublic company business outside of the boardroom that might be an inadvertent slip that could amount to an insider tip. Be careful what you say and where you say it. Keep company business discussions in the boardroom. You do not want to be involved in a case that for better or for worse may bring more clarity to the law on insider trading.

In summary, as one can see, serving on the Audit Committee of a listed company is serious business. It requires significant working knowledge of federal law and exchange rules. Almost always, this committee requires its independent directors' undivided attention to the affairs of the corporation. There is a fine line, at times, between oversight and micromanagement. Effective communication with management and the company's financial officers together with transparency in disclosures and filings will minimize loss of shareholder confidence.[37]

SUGGESTED QUESTIONS FOR THE INTERNAL AND INDEPENDENT AUDITORS

Here are a few boilerplate questions to ask the independent and internal auditors during Audit Committee meetings, depending on which questions are appropriate for the matters before the committee.

1. Is management taking any imprudent or unnecessary risks?

2. Have you had unrestricted and unlimited access to all company data, documents, records, files, and personnel in order for you to do your job?

3. Have you been made aware of any fraudulent conduct or inappropriate financial activities within the company? If so, what?

4. Have you reviewed and are you comfortable with the company's internal fiscal controls that are in place? Which ones are inadequate?

5. Have you made all the appropriate disclosures you are required to communicate to management, the Audit Committee, and the board?

6. Are you in agreement that all appropriate and required disclosures in the Q (and K) have been made? Do you feel that there are any material misrepresentations in these drafts to be filed? If so, what?

7. What is your assessment of the job the internal auditor and staff are doing? Are you communicating with them effectively? If not, why not?

8. Have you reviewed and are you in agreement with the internal audit plan?

9. Do you or does any member of your firm have any conflict of interest with the company?

10. Has your firm been sanctioned or cited for lack of compliance with any state or federal law or regulation within the last 10 years?

11. Have you been able to maintain your independence as an external audit firm throughout the course of the audit you were hired to do?

12. Has management put in place an active risk management plan, particularly with reference to financial affairs, financial controls, and financial management?

13. Are you aware of any off-balance-sheet transactions by anyone in the company or by any third party or entity involving this company? If so, what?

14. (For the internal auditors) Have you had effective and adequate communication with the independent auditors?

15. Has anyone in management tried to put any type of pressure on you or your audit staff or exert any type of influence over you or your audit staff and the results of your audit that you or any member of your staff deem inappropriate or improper?

16. Are your professional fees reasonable and necessary and consistent with industry standards? (Always review their fees and engagement letters carefully.)

17. Does the company have in place fair, timely, and confidential procedures for employees or interested parties to report to the Audit Committee any inappropriate conduct or activities by management, employees, or third parties in privities with the company? Is there a timely response to these complaints by the committee?

18. Does your firm have sufficient individuals on staff who are qualified to audit this company's information technology systems and practices? Are you performing such audits and are they incorporated into the audit plan?

19. Have you detected any deficiencies or weaknesses in the IT or cybersecurity processes or systems? If so, do any relate to internal controls or pose any financial risks?

20. Have you reviewed the Audit Committee Charter lately for any needed changes?

Of course, you will need to use the questions that pertain to your particular situation. Also, remember you are mainly focused on financial controls, financial transparency, and risk management. That does not mean you should turn a blind eye to other problems that come before the Audit Committee like safety, sexual harassment, poor marketing, information technology issues, or whatever. However, you cannot do it all, so those issues need to be referred to the appropriate committees.

Chapter 9

The Fantasyland of Executive Compensation: Directors Ought to Know How Much Is Too Much

Executive compensation is a lightning rod for today's board directors. That is because it continues to spin utterly out of control.

Hyperinflated executive salaries—most often for chief executive officers of large public companies—are the increasingly popular subjects and tantalizingly easy-to-hit targets of presidential politics. They draw the scorn of governance activists, blue-collar workers, and most sensible business people. They are appropriately skewered from all sides by the media.

One can already envision a day when new job applicants take a moment from their job interview to ask, "So, just how much is the company CEO earning these days?"

For younger workers motivated as much by the mission and purpose of organizations as by their paycheck, it is easy to understand how that one question might answer the question of whether any employer is truly living what it professes to believe as described on their websites. Pay your CEO way over the top, and it is conceivable you will be losing out in the talent wars without ever even knowing it.

A RUNAWAY TRAIN THAT IS PICKING UP STEAM

Just consider this glaring 2015 news headline: "9 CEOs Paid 800 Times More Than Their Workers" (complete with accompanying photos that might resemble a group of individual mug shots from a police lineup).[1] Only these guys are smiling—or smirking—from ear to ear.

Ridiculously high compensation schemes for the leaders of too many big American and multinational companies stand among the most visible and egregious forms of human greed and show an utter lack of oversight by too many of today's corporate boards.

They get people's blood boiling. They leave lots of smart people shaking their heads in disgust. They erode trust in the organizational mission. And to what end?

The fantasyland of executive compensation concocted by highly paid compensation consultants and fueled by companies' overreliance on external hires into the CEO role, in many cases because their directors lack the courage to promote from within or appoint someone who has not held the CEO post already with some other enterprise, continues to mystify and mortify.

Perhaps it is directors' own sense of the company's power and influence—and by extension, their own—that too often leads them to dole out incredibly lavish salaries, bonuses, perks, and retirement benefits to the leader of the enterprise. *If we are the best, and we want the best, we will pay the best.*

Too many of today's corporate board directors continue to be suckered into thinking that only one highly marketed and potentially attractive individual could possibly be qualified to tackle their company's top executive post. That is because he or she was a highly successful CEO at another company, and quite possibly in another industry, and produced terrific results for shareholders and employees.

Straight Talk: Too many of today's corporate directors are overly concerned about covering their own tails when it comes to selecting a new chief executive. They are willing to pay through the nose to land a perceived "can't miss" leader, yet they're often disappointed with the results and left footing a huge severance bill to bounce the individual when things go badly.

BIG COMPANY, BIG PROBLEM

Big-company and public company boards routinely buy into the notion—fed to them by their fellow directors, big-search-firm consultants who are especially chummy with the candidate (whom they may have recruited before), and others—that only a name-brand individual around whom there is much marketplace and social-circle mythology could possibly handle the job of leading their name-brand company.

The bigger the company, it seems, the easier it is for that company's board to buy into the hype about what it is going to take—and who it is going to take—to lead their company to its next great pinnacle.

As increasingly common board "groupthink" overwhelms the common sense of big-company boards, their directors expand the collective view of all the things the next chief executive officer must be responsible for while at the same time they narrow their view of the people who could possibly even shoulder those responsibilities.

The bigger the job, they figure, the fewer the people qualified to step into the role.

What results is a far too predictable, overly restrictive, unimaginative, and diversity-defying focus on big-name candidates who have run or are now leading similarly sized, well-known enterprises.

Oh, and it is going to take an astronomical fortune complete with sign-on incentives and golden parachute provisions in the event they're forced out to convince them to take the job. That's hogwash, but it's routinely part of the counsel boards get. Sometimes that counsel simply isn't reasonable, and often, it is simply not believable, either.

If you shrug your shoulders, wondering what you could possibly do to avoid getting steamrolled and simply give in to the arms race of CEO compensation, you are being made a fool and abandoning the best interests of your shareholders.

This is not to say that today's chief executive officers and other senior management leaders should not be handsomely paid. They should.

Particularly for the CEO's role, the job requires near-complete immersion, often requiring significant personal sacrifices in the pursuit of corporate objectives. Sometimes, family lives, marriages, and personal lives fall apart as a result. But that is no excuse for paying a king's ransom to get a highly qualified leader into that role.

Your calling as a director—particularly given the heights to which certain cases of outrageous executive compensation have risen in a national conversation on greed and failed governance—is to apply sound business judgment and reason when it comes to setting appropriate frameworks and limits for paying the CEO.

Limits, you ask? Yes. Absolutely, because these days it is not unimaginable, given the scores of ludicrous CEO pay schemes revealed in the press over the past decade, that even a disgraced and/or wholly underperforming CEO could make off with money amounting to a significant heist that could debilitate the enterprise, let alone ruin its reputation.

GREED, PURE AND SIMPLE

How much is enough for some CEOs? Well, that's just the thing.

If we have learned anything about the self-absorption of some corporate leaders and their jaw-dropping hubris and giant, uncontrolled egos, it is that there is no ceiling on what they are worth. They will take all they or their agents can sucker the board into giving—especially when they're holding the dual titles of chair and CEO.

They are holding the cards and controlling the bank, too. It is really no wonder corporate America has devolved into its current fantasyland state of literally make-believe CEO salaries, bonuses, and incentive plans. It's a fantasyland because such notions should really be confined to these CEO's imaginations.

If someone doesn't put a solid lid on the cookie jar, well, we already know what's going to happen.

> **Straight Talk:** If your CEO or any CEO candidate your board is considering expects to be the highest paid in the industry or is overly concerned with or defined by what he or she earns, show that candidate the door. Find another person willing to devote far more of his or her mindshare to driving what is good for shareholders and employees instead.

THAT IS THE DAMAGE THAT IS BEING DONE ON TOO MANY BOARDS' WATCHES

In order to make a reasonable judgment about a fair and competitive CEO compensation package, it is important for directors to consider what is in their shareholders' best interests.

Yet it is also incumbent on new and long-tenured directors to consider the significant harm that has been done and the faith and confidence that has been lost in a hail of CEO pay and severance scandals and skyrocketing CEO compensation trends.

In much the same way you will read in the following pages that the growing cyber threat is an existential one for today's employers and their boards, so, too, is the prospect of finding your CEO and the board caught in the crosshairs of a media maelstrom centered on outlandish pay practices.

That is right. Outrageously overinflated CEO pay packages rank as existential threats to the enterprise, its brand, and its future because they undermine faith and confidence in the board's leadership.

They also raise disturbing questions about whether its directors are actually in touch with reality or vested in the same CEO fantasy.

If people are asking whether your board of directors is asleep at the switch, someone had better find out what is generating that kind of skeptical inquiry—pronto. Increasingly, the genesis of those questions swirl around what the fat cats at your company are taking home for their pay.

The endemic problem that results is a wedge between management and the company's workforce. There are few issues that will ruin management relations with employees faster than the isolationism created when workers question the fairness and motivations of their leaders.

Greedy CEOs, in particular, hand their workers a bludgeon to hammer them repeatedly with—and more consequentially, the company—when reports of their compensation are revealed in public SEC filings, as required by U.S. law, or otherwise made known.

> **Straight Talk: The director's responsibility is to make his or her own judgment call about how much is too much when it comes to CEO compensation.**

Yes, the CEO must be paid very well, but if your board's definition of "very well" is perceived as "way over the moon" and simply ridiculous, your credibility will be questioned and the board's stewardship of shareholder interest will be doubted.

PUBLIC PUNCHING BAGS

CEO pay issues must absolutely scare the daylights out of corporate communications leaders. On the one hand, we do not see any of them cautioning the board about the risks of being exposed as a CEO pay poster child for bad board governance. On the other, they are exactly the folks who will be forced to jump into the fire when the media turns up the heat on a scandal involving a CEO who earns too much—especially when the company or its strategy is falling apart.

A *USA Today* analysis of CEO compensation data reported in August 2015, citing worker pay data from Glassdoor.com and CEO pay data from S&P Capital IQ, that the average CEO of Standard & Poor's 500 companies earned 216 times more than employees paid at the median average within those companies.

Adding fuel to activists' call for board intervention was the calculation that the pay gap for CEOs at nine companies—including Discovery Communications, Chipotle, and CVS Health—was 800 times the average employee's salary at their companies.[2] In the utterly reality-defying case of Discovery Communications CEO David Zaslav, his $156 million fiscal-year haul was 2,282 times greater than the average $68,397 median wage reported by *USA Today*, citing Glassdoor's data.

Then consider the impact that outrageous CEO pay schemes have in the court of public opinion. Just pick up the newspaper on any given day and there will likely be news headlines that turn investors' stomachs but also incite disgust and distrust among people left to wonder who's minding the store.

Take these, just for a few interesting examples:

- "Target Says Pay for Ousted CEO Too High"[3]
- "Restoration Hardware's Restorative CEO Comp: $66 Million"[4]
- "Time Warner Cable Guy Glenn Britt: $118m in 2013 Comp"[5]
- "Ex Wal-Mart CEO's Deferred Pay: $140 Million"[6]
- "Chesapeake Energy's McClendon Got $53 Million Severance"[7]
- "Ousted Yahoo Exec Gets $58 Million Golden Parachute"[8]
- "C.E.O. Pay Goes Up, Up and Away!"[9]

There has also been a significant spillover effect from corporate America to higher education, where salaries for some college presidents have also reached astronomical heights.

In many cases today, a big U.S. university's head football coach and/or men's basketball head coach may actually be earning more than the president or chancellor of the institution. Some big-school football and basketball coaches are now earning more than $5 million per year with at least one having reached near $10 million in one year based on incentives.

As a director, it would be particularly hard to defend a top-quartile or even industry-leading CEO pay package as outlined by the company's external compensation consultants if its pay practices across the enterprise were actually seen to be lagging those of most benchmark competitors.

There are cases, as the above news headlines determined, in which CEO pay—that combination of salary, deferred incentives, bonuses, perks, severance, and stock that can push pay issues into absurdity—can become a laughingstock. When this happens, the directors of corporate boards are seen to have been played for fools.

CEO PAY RATIOS—ADDING FUEL TO THE FIRE

It really should not have surprised anyone familiar with CEO pay practices that the United States Securities and Exchange Commission, also in August 2015, adopted a "final rule" that requires public companies to disclose the ratio of CEO pay to that of the median compensation of its employees.[10]

A statement by the SEC[11] confirmed the new pay ratio disclosure was actually mandated by the Dodd-Frank Wall Street Reform and Consumer Protection Act. Further, it explained that companies have some flexibility in calculating the pay ratio and that its purpose was also to inform shareholders when voting on so-called "say on pay."

It's important to note that U.S. public companies will be required to report the pay ratio disclosure for their first fiscal year beginning on or after January 1, 2017.[12]

When these ratios are published, they will only fan the flames of worker, political, and broader public discontent in corporate leadership. The truly corrosive effects of CEO pay will again be exposed right alongside issues like corporate tax dodges, the offshore movement of jobs, the headquartering of major corporations in far-flung tax havens, and corporate subsidies at taxpayers' expense.

Big-company directors will have an even tougher time answering questions they expect to get more and more until something is done to change the skyward momentum on CEO pay. Questions from everyday people, friends, and employees like, "Why is your CEO paid so much when many of the company's hardworking employees are struggling to survive on the measly amounts they earn?" and "How much pay is enough for our CEO?"

New directors and their longtime board peers would be wise to understand the increasing focus being put on income inequality and how runaway pay for CEOs in particular is only rubbing salt in the wound. Beyond that, truly service-minded directors will start doing something about it.

IMPLICATIONS FOR BOARD DIRECTORS

One has to wonder, especially given the public relations challenges looming just over the corporate governance horizon because of inexplicable CEO pay packages, whether the risks to corporate brands, investor relations, and employee morale are really worth it.

How would any board—and any director, for that matter—respond to any other issue that threatens to undo long-standing relationships and trusted bonds with shareholders? To what extent would a director care that employee morale—and perhaps relationships with worker unions— might be torpedoed overnight by news that the CEO is essentially robbing the place blind?

Remove the words "CEO compensation" from the equation, and lots of directors would take a stand in defense of the company, in defense of shareholders and their corporate brand, and in the spirit of effective risk management. Yet, for some reason, one you start fiddling with the issue of CEO pay, these same instincts seem to take a back seat in favor of personal politics and going along with the team.

But this is one issue that has risen to existential levels. As a director, you have got to take stock of the beating your organization may take or is taking based on its decision to lavishly compensate the CEO—the very leader an increasing number of voices would agree should be oriented more to service than to his or her own wealth creation.

So what does all this really mean for new directors and those already serving on boards?

It means you ought to expect and perhaps brace for more transparency regarding what the organization's senior leaders are earning, particularly in public companies. It means that you as a director may need to become better versed in how CEO compensation is constructed and why. It means you will be getting more questions about equity and why workers at the entry level and in some job functions are struggling to survive on less than a living wage.

It means that compensation practices are going to remain part of every director's vernacular. It may also portend more annual shareholders' meetings dominated by say on pay, discussions (and heated exchanges) about CEO compensation, and more discovery into why shareholders aren't getting their fair share.

Something else directors must understand is that, so long as their succession options are heavily geared toward or immediately biased by the preconception that only an outsider will suffice as the company's next CEO, they will contribute to the steady escalation of CEO pay.

A large part of the reason why CEO pay has skyrocketed is the premium of 20 to 30 percent or more that boards are told they have to pay in order to attract a highly qualified candidate. In some cases, the premium to land the big-name candidate is even higher. The (flawed) thinking is that no self-respecting CEO would dare step into a role that would pay less than what his or her predecessor earned.

So, right from the start, too many CEO packages have as their starting low point the compensation package the last guy or gal in the role had, then almost immediately graduate up by some premium multiple to recognize perceptions (often significant misconceptions) about the quality of the candidate the board wants to select.

During the process, those very perceptions are often fanned by the executive recruiter leading the search, reinforced by the compensation consultants, structured by specialist lawyers who are experts at executive employment agreements, and finalized in part when directors buy into everything they hear as gospel.

With no ceiling and in many cases no director challenging the reasonableness of what is being offered to the incoming CEO, the compensation gravy train gathers steam and sometimes leads the company off the tracks. The fox, it seems at that point, is deeply entrenched in the hen house.

For these reasons, and many others, pay for performance, also known as P4P, has been gaining momentum in the United States.

Linking a greater percentage of CEO compensation to the actual results the CEO has helped to achieve is a step in the right direction.

It is important to remind us all, right there, that no one person drives results alone.

The CEO sets the tone and crafts the strategy—with significant help and guidance, including from the board. The CEO's behavior makes organizational culture real or a laughingstock among employees huddled in whispers in the break room or at the water cooler. And now, we can all agree, the CEO's pay says a lot about how the place is being governed, and who is really in control.

It will be up to a new generation of corporate directors to put a stop to the madness. But control over the board nominating process will be key to ushering in that change. So long as that process is controlled from the inside, sensible CEO pay reform will be difficult to achieve because of cronyism-based director selection.

Straight Talk: Those who control the board nominating process hold the keys to CEO pay reform.

Chapter 10

Cybersecurity Is Every Director's Business: Why Cyberattacks Are Existential Threats

It is the subject of an increasing number of hushed conversations between corporate directors.

"How bad was it, really?" "When did you first find out?" "How did your board respond?"

It is a growing concern and one you need to understand without delay.

Just consult today's business news and you will likely find a quick example. Then check again tomorrow and the next day for further proof.

And it is very much your business even if you do not know much about modern-day technology.

It is a malicious breach of or series of repeated attacks against your organization's corporate data that can happen overnight and without warning, and that can cast the company and its board into an existential crisis perhaps faster than any other threat possibly could.

It is a breach or consistent, malicious campaign of attacks that could be described in one of many ways, perhaps as a denial of service attack, a state-sponsored attack, a "back door" to infiltrate typical authentication procedures, spoofing, or a Trojan attack.

Straight Talk: If you do not know what the enterprise is doing to thwart the potential of such cyberattacks, it is high time you did.

As today's enterprises generate more and more data on customers, suppliers, employees, and global business partners, computer technology or information technology (IT) infrastructure—and the security mechanisms meant to safeguard it—has become an integral component of everyday business operations and an increasing budget item.

The value of the information architecture now supporting the global economy likely runs into the trillions of dollars. The value of intellectual property, proprietary software and systems, and all the enterprise functions they support within any individual organization likely ranks among its top assets and individual budget lines. Corporate spending on IT systems and security safeguards is massive and getting bigger all the time—for good reason.

Organizations spend heavily to create enterprise software, databases, networks, and computer infrastructure that make their teams more productive, more efficient, and better prepared to meet shifting customer or consumer needs, from their office desktops or their mobile phones and related "on-the-go" handheld devices.

Companies of all sizes now warehouse massive amounts of data that include patent technology, confidential financial data and privileged executive-level communications, customer credit card information, customer profiles, and other information like Social Security numbers and passwords that criminal elements want to infiltrate.

UNDERSTANDING THE CYBER ENVIRONMENT

The Honorable Dale Meyerrose, Major General, United States Air Force (retired), was the first president-appointed, Senate-confirmed chief information officer and information sharing executive for the U.S. intelligence community. He was director of Command Control Systems for the North American Aerospace Defense Command during the events of September 11, 2001, and together with his team helped safeguard the air sovereignty of North America.

Meyerrose is widely recognized as one of the world's leading experts on the intersection of leadership, cyber, information technology, security, intelligence, and military matters. His expertise and counsel is valued by boards of directors, conference keynote organizers, and media worldwide.

Today, as president of the MeyerRose Group LLC, based in Colorado Springs, he consults with a wide range of business, government, and academic institutions on strategy, technology, education, and executive development issues. Meyerrose is also an associate professor at the School of Information Studies at Syracuse University.

Meyerrose says that before board directors and aspiring directors for companies, not-for-profit organizations, and other entities can fully understand how to protect institutional data, they must first comprehend how information has in many ways become its central nervous system and such a valuable differentiator.

"With cyber," Meyerrose says, "we talk a lot about losing this and losing that, but people don't want to stop buying retail, doing their banking, and using social networking because there's a belief that the positive far outweighs the negative. And they are right. The art of the possible trumps the fear of the inevitable. But these positives also create new vulnerabilities."

Cyber is the word he and others use to describe the medium or infrastructure upon which data flows, giving meaning to the modern-day focus on cybersecurity.

For example, Meyerrose cites his own handheld. He doesn't call it a cell phone, because most of what he uses it for has nothing to do with the device's functionality as a phone. Rather, it seamlessly integrates GPS (global positioning satellite) data, a Web browser, applications to monitor his heart and how many steps he takes in a day, what's happening with the stock market, and other useful things like notifications that he's about to be picked up at the airport.

When businesspeople the world over use their handheld devices in the same ways, they are doing so outside the company firewall. "We started with the computer, then changed the language to reflect a system, and then we talked about IT (information technology), and now it's cyber. Cyber is the medium," Meyerrose says.

"In each case, we've changed language to match the context and the medium's ubiquity and utility. The reason we talk about cyber or IT security or information security is because most of the workforce operates outside the firewall and they're on the move, they're on their mobile devices, their iPads and wireless networks," he explains.

Often, employees are using these devices to access information that is not stored in a corporate database, but rather part of open-sourced data far beyond the reaches of their employers' computer or network security protection. "The notion of information security has been around for decades," he says, "but cybersecurity in today's context is all about protecting organizational interests that are off-campus."

Meyerrose says that much of an organization's growth today hinges on its ability to maximize its distinct information advantage. "It's really all about the art of the possible and maximizing that because you're looking for enablers, multipliers of capability. Companies use cyber to penetrate markets, to send mass emails, and to do an increasing share of their marketing. It's important to start with understanding the full impact that cyber has on the organization."

The context and nuance about how people are using information to get their jobs done is important. Meyerrose says that is because as we stretch the meaning of safe computing and as organizations put their focus on deploying safe systems, hiring the right people, training them correctly, and ensuring they follow procedures, it is equally important to understand what evildoers can do to us, and what we need to do to protect ourselves has likewise evolved and changed.

TWO CRITICAL LESSONS FOR DIRECTORS AND EFFECTIVE CYBER GOVERNANCE

When it comes to cyber matters, it is essential for today's sitting and future directors to understand two things very clearly. *First, cyber attacks represent existential threats, and second, they demand your focus, preparation, and response no matter how comfortable you as a director are with technology.*

Further to point one above, cybersecurity is not just a data issue or something that should be compartmentalized as a purely technology issue for the tech guys and gals to figure out when something goes wrong. Cyber is all around us. **When things go wrong, the threat is existential to the entire organization, not just to its technology platform or most qualified IT people.**

"I believe the single most important element about cybersecurity and where it ranks among board directors' priorities is that it's not a separate, technical thing. It is wholly an enterprise-level issue. It should be a real existential concern to every director and officer of the company. Cybersecurity issues exist in the context of the outside world, not solely in cybersecurity terms," Meyerrose explains.

"The reason any cyber attack is existential is because what it's threatening is vitally important—the valuable, proprietary data and systems infrastructure of the organization and the productivity of all the people who rely on it to do their jobs. It's part of the basic fabric of things that are critical to the organization's success and sustainability," Meyerrose shares.

If it threatens how the entire enterprise operates, it is indeed existential and rises to an organizational crisis. It is as serious as having your headquarters building on fire or the CEO dying suddenly. It very much calls for an all-hands response, not just a call to the IT Department. "If your building is on fire," Meyerrose illustrates, "you wouldn't only call your facilities manager and say, 'Go take care of that fire.' You might be inclined to call the 'tech guys' in the event of a cyberattack, but you might be asking them to fix something that has nothing to do with their systems. You better get everyone in your organization engaged to answer the call."

> **Straight Talk: Cyberattacks are an existential threat. Treat them as such.**

The cybersecurity threat is not just a data issue. It may threaten the confidence of investors and put the organization's brand at risk. It may threaten the loss of intellectual property, the safety of people, and the future of the organization. It may also come from a surprising source.

In fact, at least 90 percent of cyberattacks have a low-tech genesis, starting out in some nontech domain and ultimately migrating to cyber.

"The cyber predators don't attack with cyber. They typically attack with a theft. Consider the employee who lost a laptop or other piece of equipment with critical files on it, or the fact that someone may have left a vulnerability on a Web page, or someone got tricked or conned into giving up their security credentials," Meyerrose says.

That theft often enables the bad guys to gain access to IT infrastructure that enables them to start attacking from behind or inside the firewall. "Organizations need to be looking inward," Meyerrose asserts.

He compares that paradigm shift to the one that changed the U.S. military's view of protecting the homeland after the 9/11 attacks. Before that terrible day, leadership was focused on the threat of an external threat, so its defense mechanisms were arrayed accordingly. However, in the wake of 9/11, there was a realization that the nation had to evaluate potential outside incursions but also look inside for effective air defenses.

"You have to apply the same kind of thinking with cyber. You have to look inside. You have to consider the high probability that authorized people may be doing something stupid, unauthorized, and/or inadvertently that opens you up for cyberattack," Meyerrose says. "More than 90 percent of all cyber attacks are traced to insiders. They opened an email they shouldn't have, they lost track of something that had valuable data on it. The rate of purposeful insider attacks is noteworthy but still quite low."

Once perpetrators have infiltrated a target organization's database, website, or IT systems, they then engage ever more sophisticated techniques to exploit their infiltration. Meyerrose prefers the term "infiltration" to "hack," which from his view suggests that someone is breaking and entering as a burglar would do to an insecure home. "If someone answers the door and allows someone in, is that breaking and entering?" Meyerrose asks to prove his point.

"When they get inside or behind the firewall," he adds, "they use whatever works. It could be three or four different things. It's not just one tool. Think of a bank heist in which one guy blows a hole in the wall, another guy drives the getaway car, and another guy undoes the electronic lock or inserts a banking spider that knows the money isn't in the bank but in a site vault."

Still, with cyberattacks, most of the means engaged are decidedly low-tech and unsophisticated at first. Then the information is ultimately passed to another criminal element that knows how to exploit the stolen data or exploit the infiltration.

> **Straight Talk:** Someone on the board has to have accountability, responsibility, and oversight for anything that touches cybersecurity. You need a point person on the board who can help assess a cyberattack or longer-term campaign of attacks and provide the leadership to understand the source of the problem and what has to be done on an enterprise level to stop it.

The second point from above is that, even if you're a director who doesn't use email or a computer (we know you are out there, and you are fewer and fewer in number each day), **your own lack of familiarity with or sense of confidence working with computers, network systems, and all things digital in no way excuses you from making a valuable contribution to important cybersecurity dialogue around the boardroom table. In fact, your experience in weighing risks (such as investment risks), assessing them, and assigning the right resources to mitigate those risks might be crucial to effective governance in the event of a cyberattack.**

Too often, board directors who are not all that comfortable with computers, email, handheld mobile devices, and the like get bamboozled into thinking they could not possibly add anything to a serious discussion of cybersecurity, how to prevent attacks, and how to respond when they do happen.

But that dog won't hunt.

Any director worth his or her salt knows how to make sound business judgments about things like enterprise vulnerabilities, risks, and opportunities. Well, since cyber *is* business, although you may not understand what a Trojan attack is or a waterfall defense strategy, because you understand risk and how to calculate it and make judgments about maximizing product or service while mitigating risk, you likely already have exactly what it takes to help navigate through a cyber infiltration.

Any director who says he or she cannot understand this stuff simply has not tried hard enough. It is far less about bits and bytes and far more about dollars and sense. It is about evaluating risks and benefits. If you are the tech-savvy director on your board, you owe it to your fellow board peers to make it translatable to them. If you cannot do it, engage the organization's chief risk officer or chief financial officer or chief information officer or chief technology officer to put it all in plain talk—including dollars and cents—which every director will be able to figure out.

The complexity and regularity of massive data breaches is a subject of increasing concern among today's boards and also of increasing investment to ensure the company's cybersecurity systems and protocols are at least one step ahead of data thieves' own increasing sophistication.

Yet there are also significant internal threats to enterprise data, and other in-house challenges that can point to additional technological vulnerabilities that organizations—and their boards of directors—must not only be aware of but significantly prepared to address if they are ultimately realized.

Again, let us consider employees' use of laptop computers, smartphones, and other connected devices that could be used as a platform for malware or as a vehicle for their own illicit activities. They say an email never dies.

That's why it is important for board directors and executives to remember that if they must engage in a highly privileged or otherwise sensitive, confidential discussion, it is always better to do it face-to-face than to have an email intercepted by or delivered to unintended recipients.

> **Straight Talk: Unless you are willing to testify to it, do not ever put something of a highly sensitive, confidential, and/or otherwise privileged nature in an email. It could fall into the wrong hands, and it could come back to haunt you.**

THE CALL FOR BETTER CYBERSECURITY

Two things stand out when it comes to assessing cyberattacks against major corporate data infrastructure.

The first is that some attacks go unnoticed and unreported by the press (remember that private companies large and small have no duty to publicly report these infiltrations), thereby complicating the job of uncovering their perpetrators.

The second is that, often, the initial indications of the true scale of a cyber breach (often of data in the custody of publicly traded companies and government agencies) are underreported, with the full scale of the damage not revealed until weeks or months later as investigators conduct detailed forensics on the breach, its source, and its likely or demonstrated illegal agents.

In 2014 alone, there were 61,000 cyberattacks against the United States government alone, according to Meyerrose. And let us not forget perhaps the most publicized cyber infiltration against the U.S. government—that by insider Edward Snowden, the man who leaked classified information from the U.S. National Security Agency in 2013.

Also of note, an estimated 70 percent of existing Web pages can be exploited very easily, by Meyerrose's calculations. Cyber criminals can target these sites' privileged users and cause chaos as a result.

All of this points to the need for significant awareness and preparedness, not only among board directors, but also among C-suite executives and most especially the chief IT officer, be that a chief technology officer or chief information officer. In a small but growing number of enterprises, the responsibility for keeping the bad guys at bay falls to none other than an appointed chief cybersecurity officer, sometimes also referred to as a chief information security officer.

At the time of this writing, one professional networking site had fewer than 150 members as part of its working network group. We expect these numbers—and the importance of that role—to swell quickly as the global business community comes to terms with the growing severity—and increasing cost—of this escalating existential threat.

> **Straight Talk: As a director, you should ensure that the cybersecurity buck stops with just one person. Do not settle for a "committee approach" to effective cybersecurity. Push the CEO—if necessary—to make cybersecurity job number one for someone in the enterprise. Get to know that individual and learn what he or she is doing to prevent cyberattacks. You will be glad you did.**

The growing list of companies that have been victimized by these digital delinquents is alarming. Things have gotten to the point where, in just a few years' time, it may be tougher to name the big-name corporate brands that haven't been hit by a major cyberattack—or perhaps, whose data breaches haven't been splashed all over the business media.

There is enough in the public body of knowledge about the seriousness of cybersecurity that today's directors—and tomorrow's board candidates—should already consider cybertheft one of the devils they know or should know. It is an emerging threat, and one that hits closer to home when one delves into the companies that got caught in the crosshairs, and the fact that you may be a customer or constituent of one of them.

MEMORABLE CYBERATTACKS

Target

In late 2013, Target Corporation (NYSE: TGT), an upscale discount retailer with nearly 1,800 stores and 38 distribution centers in the United States as of August 2015, revealed that 110 million customer credit card and debit card accounts were hacked during the peak holiday shopping season. Had the attack happened in February 2013 instead, Meyerrose surmises, "no one would have known."

It stands today as one of the largest data breaches ever reported, although it may not hold that unenviable ranking much longer as these crimes continue to multiply in scope and means.

Hackers breached the company's payment system by reportedly stealing computer log-ins from a vendor that performed heating and air-conditioning services for Target stores.[1] All told, these computer data thieves made off with 40 million credit card numbers and personal information from 70 million online accounts.

The attack was linked in media reports to overseas hackers, and a single blogger was credited with breaking news of the cyberattack after discovering a flood of credit cards reaching underground markets that sell stolen credit card data.[2]

Investigators determined that the Target attack was actually a coordinated malware assault against multiple U.S. retailers at the same time, and one that inserted a virus that yanked critical customer data between the prime business hours of 10 a.m. and 5 p.m., which helped conceal the malware.[3]

The financial impact for the company's bottom line was clear and immediate. Traffic into Target's stores decreased and its profit for the quarter dropped 46 percent. Consumers temporarily lost confidence in their ability to safely use credit cards at the company's checkout counters, Meyerrose says. "That's why the Target CEO and CIO got fired," he adds.

Target ultimately paid $10 million to settle a class-action lawsuit brought by shoppers claiming they were impacted by the hack.[4]

In August 2015, Target reached a deal with Visa (NYSE: V) to pay its card issuers what the *Wall Street Journal* and other media reported as a maximum $67 million to settle the retailer's massive data breach.[5] An earlier tentative agreement with MasterCard reportedly was not accepted by enough of its card issuers.

In a statement at the time of the Visa deal forecasting its own ramped-up investment in cybersecurity controls and infrastructure, Visa announced: "This agreement attempts to put this event behind us, and increase the industry's focus on protecting against future compromises with new technologies."

Meyerrose, by the way, says that although the Target cyber infiltration may have generated the most headlines at the end of 2013, it actually only ranked about 11th on the list of that year's biggest cyberattacks.

It's really no wonder why the cybersecurity industry is beginning to boom. Every organization with custody of sensitive customer, member, or affiliate data now has a heightened duty to protect that data, and plenty of examples of what can go wrong if they don't.

Straight Talk: Your board should engage with your company's top cybersecurity expert on a regular basis. And if your board doesn't already include someone with deep technology expertise, it should.

Internal Revenue Service

A hack of the Internal Revenue Service's online Get Transcript service, which allowed users to review a record of their tax account transactions, reportedly compromised personal identity–related data on some 334,000 taxpayers,[6] three times its initial May 2015 estimate.

The IRS pointed out that these were taxpayer accounts that were subject to unauthorized access, and it couldn't by August 2015 determine whether information was actually stolen from each of them.

In this particular case, the breach was an authentication crime through which the bad guys gathered information about taxpayers from other sources and correctly used it to answer a number of identity verification questions tied to the Get Transcript service.

This is a particularly egregious criminal activity because the data thieves who were cloaked in the digital appearance of actual taxpayers and the Get Transcript system didn't have any other way to authenticate who was actually accessing taxpayer data.

The IRS promised to send letters to the taxpayers whose information was illegally accessed. It also pledged to provide them free credit protection and identity protection personal identification numbers or PINS for future access to their records.

But there were two other elements to this cyberhack story that merit repeating as they underscore the growing severity of the problem and the financial toll it is exacting, in these cases, on the American public.

The IRS, just one of many federal government agencies struggling to deal with these threats, started tracking the number of attempted—but not successful—incursions into its data. In May 2015, the IRS reported a total of 111,000 suspected cybertheft attempts on taxpayer accounts. Just three months later, it reported an additional 170,000 attempts to break through its digital barriers for the purpose of stealing taxpayer data.

Further, the IRS stopped 19 million suspicious tax returns and protected more than $63 billion in fraudulent tax refunds, according to one *Forbes* report.[7]

The IRS has actually worked to inform taxpayers about the most popular scams through which criminal elements are trying to access things like names, physical addresses, Social Security numbers, and tax records. It publishes what it calls its "Dirty Dozen Tax Scams" to brief taxpayers on the different ways these crooks are trying to scam the government, and in some cases, attempting to directly mislead and victimize individual taxpayers.

The other disturbing aspect to this cybersecurity case study is the fact that, according to a Government Accountability Office (GAO) report,[8] the IRS paid out an estimated $5.8 billion worth of tax refunds to hackers in 2013 who used other people's information to file fraudulent tax returns in their names. The good news in an otherwise alarming story is that the same GAO report found that the IRS prevented illegal tax refund payments totaling an estimated $24.2 billion from going to the wrong hands.

Ashley Madison

"Life is short. Have an affair."

That's how Ashley Madison, which is based in Canada and owned by Avid Life Media, a company that describes itself as a social entertainment company that has launched multiple online dating sites, invited what it claims was a collection of 39 million "anonymous members"[9] to create an account. Users could browse the site for free but would have to enter credit card numbers to pay for the right to contact other purported members.[10]

Given the site's slogan, it's natural to suspect most of those who signed up and trolled the website were married people.

What is probably more clear is that few if any of them figured the names, credit card numbers, email addresses, physical addresses, and sexual preferences they shared with the site—and, in the case of those preferences, with other users—would ultimately be stolen in July 2015 and later posted on a remote corner of the Internet by hackers who stole the data on what they claimed were 32 million Ashley Madison accounts.

The perpetrators posted the Ashley Madison user data on what is known as the "Dark Web," a part of the Internet that can only be accessed through a browser called Tor. It cannot be accessed via some of the most popular search engines such as Google. The data, however, could apparently be copied and pasted from that deep Internet domain to virtually anyplace on the Web.

The hackers, who called themselves the Impact Team, also mocked the site's users, noting with some level of perceived impunity that some 90 percent to 95 percent of its users were actually male. The site has reportedly been challenged on the basis that many of its female profiles were faked.[11]

The Ashley Madison hack was, for some, personally devastating, and for far more people, highly instructive about the consequences of information insecurity and the perils of sharing too much of one's private life online.

Just consider this subsequent headline from the *Toronto Star*: "Ashley Madison Hack May Be Linked to Hate Crimes, Extortion, Suicide, Police Say."[12]

Toronto police said the hacking of the adultery website may have led to what was reported as extortion attempts and two unconfirmed suicides related to the release of personal user information.

Some of those listed as Ashley Madison users at the time of the August 2015 posting of the stolen data were being threatened with exposure and potential humiliation if they did not pay money to extortionists. The serious nature of the case ultimately moved Avid Life Media to offer a reward of CA$500,000 or roughly US$380,000 for information leading to the arrest of those who perpetrated the cyberattack.[13]

In multiple other cases, employees of a wide variety of companies, government agencies, and other organizations were subject to internal personnel investigations because they might have violated workplace email and communications policies forbidding the personal use of work email, computers, and network systems.

Victims of the data leak filed lawsuits in the United Kingdom and the United States, invoking a claim to anonymity. Some well-known television personalities, as well as business executives with well-known global companies, sports teams, and government agencies were outed, with some of them moved to publicly acknowledge their transgressions. The Toronto police even put out a call to the hacking community to expose the Impact Team because of what it termed "enormous social and economic fallout."[14]

What is more, one antivirus software developer claimed that the Ashley Madison cyberaffair was not a hack at all, and rather, was perpetrated as an inside job by a disgruntled Ashley Madison employee.[15]

> **Straight Talk: Anything you do or say online may be tracked. If your company cannot prevent a hack or insider data breach, you as a director of the company should inform your board peers that it should already be saving toward its legal defense fund.**

U.S. Office of Personnel Management

While not nearly as sordid as the Ashley Madison case, the data breach of the files of the federal Office of Personnel Management (OPM) was no less alarming for those sounding the call to effective defenses and preparedness against cyberattacks.

Reports in June 2015 revealed a massive security lapse, potentially exposing the federal employment records of as many as four million current and former government workers to criminal elements. However, an investigation revealed that the data stolen may have actually affected 21.5 million federal employees and civilians.[16]

At the time, Meyerrose says, the OPM infiltration ranked as the largest cyberattack of 2015. But by the end of that year, it was outstripped in size by well more than 100 other cyberattacks.

It would surprise few to learn than a 2014 audit of OPM's data management and protection practices discovered security flaws in the agency's information systems, yet the issues surfaced were reportedly not divulged until several months later. A cited "material weakness" in OPM's data systems had been downgraded to a "significant deficiency" by 2014, yet a lack of action left its data vulnerable.

The hack was initially blamed on Chinese hackers,[17] but the Obama administration ultimately sidestepped the potential international repercussions of such a direct allegation or attribution of state-sponsored cybercrime by a foreign government.

The administration decided against publicly blaming China out of concern for how its foreign intelligence sources and the evidence they collected—as well as its own cyber countermeasures—could be compromised if it were to make such a public allegation of China's involvement.[18]

The depth of this cyberattack was significant. The hackers—whoever they were—gained access to security clearance information and background checks dating back to the mid-1980s. They may have also gained valuable intelligence about critical weapons systems, according to at least one report.[19] And this was reportedly the second breach of OPM systems in less than a year.

We can expect the federal government—and governmental agencies around the world—to help fuel the continued expansion of the global cybersecurity market for some years to come. As a director, it is your job to ensure your company is competing for the best and brightest minds in the cyberdefense world, and actually adding them as key assets to thwart this growing operational and information governance concern.

Sony Pictures Entertainment

In November 2014, two years after a breach by so-called "hacktivists," Sony Pictures saw some of its confidential data compromised by cyber criminals, including personal information about Sony Pictures employees and their families, emails between employees, and information about executive salaries. Meyerrose says it all started out as an attempt at blackmail.

There was a claim of responsibility for the attack by a group calling themselves "Guardians of Peace" or "GOP." Embarrassing email correspondence, in which company executives mocked the president and some Hollywood celebrities, was made public. So, too, came a demand that the company cancel its plans to release a controversial movie, *The Interview*, a so-called "comedy" about a plot to assassinate sitting North Korean leader Kim Jong Un. There was also an attempt to wipe the company's workstations and servers.

Some claimed that North Korea was behind it all, intent to derail distribution of the movie. The Federal Bureau of Investigation investigated whether the North Koreans could be linked to the cyberattack.[20] The

Korean Central News Agency, a state-run media outlet, responded but called reports of its involvement "wild rumor."[21]

The movie was ultimately released, and the North Koreans denied any involvement, but President Obama signed an executive order in early January 2015 imposing tougher sanctions on the isolated North Korean regime in direct response to the cyberattack on Sony Pictures.[22]

"Every crisis has got multiple facets," Meyerrose says. "This one," he says, "all started out with blackmail." Meyerrose and other noted cybersecurity experts have cast doubt on whether the attack was perpetrated by the North Koreans.

CLOSING THOUGHTS ON CYBER

When board directors appreciate all the benefits their companies are getting from cyber assets and start looking at cyber risks as if they were investment risks, they begin to understand cyber assets' value and why they must be protected. They also remove the conjured psychological distress of feeling underqualified to contribute to effective information governance.

Cyber could be looked at like a public company's responsibility to file timely and accurate financial reports with the Securities and Exchange Commission (SEC). If your company were to file them with significant inaccuracies and/or with malicious intent, you could go to jail and sink the entire organization. Likewise with cyber, if your cyber strategy, assets, and operations aren't handled correctly, it can put everything at risk of collapse—including lots of careers.

One of your jobs as a director—one of increasing focus for many boards—is to maximize all the enterprise is getting from its cyber assets. If the organization is truly doing that, calculating the risk of exposure to cyber infiltration becomes easier.

How much of the board's agenda should be apportioned for discussion about effective information security? There are budgetary standards in each industry, and so it all depends on the industry space your enterprise is in and the comfort level your fellow board members have in feeling risks have been mitigated as much as can be reasonably expected in times like these.

One of the things you can do as a director is to understand your organization's commitment—financial and operational—to meeting the cyber challenge. Also, you can make some level of cyber competency a requirement for your current and next chief executive.

One of the lessons from some of the government cases cited herein is to give your employees answers to these questions: "If I suspect a cyber infiltration or theft, whom do I report that to and how?" and "Who should be in contact with the authorities?" and "What should we be telling our people?" and "How best should we advise them so they don't make any crisis worse?" Of course, there are also matters involving partners, customers, vendors, and, if applicable, shareholders and regulators in the event of a malicious cyber event.

"They all have to know what to think if the worst happens," Meyerrose says. "If it's catastrophic enough, they have to know they're not going to get any service, especially if you run a point of sale in the retail business, for example."

Postattack, as a director it is up to you to ensure your company is not just patching a hole in its cyber infrastructure. Rather, the hole has to be changed so it is not as exploitable as it was before.

Remember, this is an existential enterprise threat. Your board's goal—and that of your organization's operating executive team—should not simply be to restore operations, but rather, to create a new normal or a new cyber normal for the institution that is less penetrable than before. You have to restore things to a whole new state in order to really feel secure once again.

> **Straight Talk: Cyber is a risk like any investment risk. If you make the wrong investment, the organization can lose its assets, along with its reputation, financial support, and market momentum. As a director, it is partly up to you to ensure that does not happen.**

Chapter 11

The Leadership That Boards Need Now: The Most Critical Dynamics on Today's Boards Are Human Ones

The operating environment for today's directors and boards—corporate, not-for-profit, institutional, and governmental—is more fast-paced, more global, and more closely watched than ever before. They face pressure from all sides in the form of regulators, shareholders, activists, and media.

This increasingly transparent and externally influenced governance landscape is also full of opportunities to provide these stakeholders and the communities our organizations serve renewed confidence in effective governance oversight.

The leadership that boards need now is very much attainable. But it will only be realized if directors fully understand the seriousness of their duty. Directors must commit to investing the time required to learn the key issues. They must stand their ground on matters of ethics and risk management. And they must challenge and stretch one another to keep an open mind no matter what expertise or experience they bring to the boardroom.

Today's boards need leaders who are experienced enough to inspire confidence in their abilities and self-aware enough to recognize the limits of their knowledge, time, and energy. Their memberships need to become more diverse, not only to align with the meritocracy they espouse, but also to connect more authentically with the global populations they serve.

Directors must be acutely aware—at all times—about how perceptions of their connectedness with issues faced by consumers, employees, shareholders, and others contribute to the well-being and sustainability of their organizations.

These exact issues will no doubt be cast into the public spotlight with even more frequency when the CEO Pay Ratio Rule, required by the Dodd-Frank financial reform act of 2010, shines a bright light on CEO compensation as a multiple of the median total compensation earned by their employees in the spring of 2018.

If you are the director of a company with an exceptionally high-paid CEO but a dismal track record of performance and return to shareholders, you had better buckle up. It is going to get real stormy out there and you better be prepared by examining the rationale for that CEO pay ratio real fast.

As with so many things in life and effective board stewardship, things often boil down to a judgment call.

A decision should be made with the best of intentions, clarity of internal perspective and external intelligence, and the fortitude to stand behind your decision. Many directors chalk this up to having their conscience speak to them, or that little voice inside their head that calls an alarm when something does not look or smell just right. Others call it "common sense." Still others, "guts," "conviction," or even "courage."

The leadership boards need will come in many forms. It will assuredly come in the form of an active, discerning Audit Committee with the courage and commitment to set the record straight when things don't go as planned.

It will reveal itself in board Nominating/Governance Committee practices that reflect a commitment to attain the right leadership competencies rather than perpetuate the historically insular or chummy board appointment patterns that have turned the "who" into the end goal and therein enabled ridiculous executive compensation practices.

And it will come from Executive Compensation Committees whose members know where to draw a reasoned line in the sand beyond which no CEO is worth paying, not because limits are right but because shareholders must not be fleeced.

DO YOUR JOB

As a board director, it is incumbent on you to do your homework, plain and simple. Prepare for board meetings. Read the materials ahead of time. Show up and contribute meaningfully to the dialogue when you have something important to share.

And for goodness' sake, do not ever doze off during a board meeting. If you do, you will invite distrust and your reputation will take a hit and impact future relations with your board peers. Be ready, well rested, and bring a positive attitude and an open, inquiring mind.

The word "inquiring" here is worth particular noting.

All through the pages of this book, we have shared real-world stories, practical ideas, and experience-driven insights about what it means to be a good director on any board.

Yet it is very important to emphasize that in today's governance and regulatory environment, simply checking the box on your job description as a director may not be enough to keep you in good standing with your peers and the organization you are serving. Heck, it may not even be enough to keep you out of jail.

There is increasing fluidity in the requirements of a good board director. New risks are realized at a dizzying pace. The complexity of doing business globally brings its own challenge. And then come the priorities driven by regulators, customers, employees, unions, shareholders, and more.

What this means is that, in addition to doing your homework, you must be proactive about poking your nose around the place, looking for trouble, and connecting the things you see as potential risks and opportunities to management practices, organizational practices and policies, and the means to reduce enterprise risk.

One of the continuing failings of boards today is that there is reliance on too many cookie-cutter approaches and solutions, be they related to board self-evaluations, cybersecurity, investigating due diligence, or succession for both the CEO and the board.

After all, just because your organization's lawyers and financial people say they are actively assessing and managing enterprise risk doesn't mean your board—and your own backside—is not exposed.

There are significant risks associated with almost every strategic decision that comes before the board. Your job as a director is to consider and weigh in on the risks that someone brings to the board's table, but also to inquire, probe, and ask for answers to questions when you yourself see other risks just under the surface.

Straight Talk: Get into the habit of asking, "What is the worst that could happen?" and "What can and are we doing to prevent that?" If you do not get a good answer, go in search of your own answers and report your findings back to the board.

More often than not, you will get some answers to that question, although in many instances, they will be flimsy answers that in no way elevate your assuredness that everything will turn out just fine. It is in these cases that you need to commit to exploring potential risk areas on your own, perhaps saving a deeper discussion about any particular risk or possible risk for another day.

The point here is that you can easily—although with a lot of work—move from one board meeting agenda to another and get a lot done with your board colleagues while at the same time fail to see something big that's lurking just around the corner.

Yes, maybe the makings of a good director in times like ours mean that there is some level of healthy paranoia about enterprise risk and risk exposure.

There will be risks to nearly everything the organization does—risks associated with new ventures and financial investments and hedges, risks relating to people and leaders and business partners, and most certainly there will be potential peril in transactions such as mergers and acquisitions (particularly on the often overlooked topics of postdeal leadership and workforce culture integration).

Because it is your job to provide effective governance oversight for the organization, it is also your job as a board director to make sure someone is evaluating the business risks of key strategic decisions and transactions. That is the key—leave no stone unturned. Be diligent, vigilant, and persistent, even if that means revealing yourself as a pain in someone else's neck.

Now all this does not mean you should become a Chicken Little on your board. The last thing you need is a reputation as someone who is panic-prone or committed to finding the fault in everything.

But what is really important is that others see you doing your job. Asking tough questions. Probing for risks and weaknesses that competitors or perhaps even criminal elements could exploit. Doing your own research on these issues, and asking others to do theirs so there are no surprises. If you do these things, you will do your job as a director and do it well.

DO NOT BE FOOLED

If you have applied good judgment and invested enough due diligence in the right places, you should be in good standing with the board you serve and the peers you serve with.

But there may come a time when you will get a sense that someone is trying to pull one over on the board, or put one past the goaltender—

almost hoping the board hasn't done its homework or does not probe too deeply on a particular issue.

This is when it is important to examine motivations. Whether it is during the interviewing of a prospective CEO hire or in kicking the tires on a new investment decision (something like board portals, for example), it is important to dig in and find out what you're really being sold. It is your job to separate the wheat from the chaff.

On matters like CEO succession, you cannot afford to be fooled. Before handing the keys of executive management to anyone, you had better get to know the person, find out what is really important to him or her, understand specifically about how his or her experience relates to your organization's mission and objectives, and stand independently on your own takeaways on those vital measures. Compare your view of the individual to the views of others. Recalibrate, probe, and collaborate to find consensus.

But there are a host of other issues that will compete for your time and attention as a director—and undoubtedly fill your email inbox—and it is up to you to determine what is important and what is really nothing more than a distraction.

Governance trends and "topics of the day" are sweeping across directors' desks, computers, and mobile devices faster and in a greater volume than ever before. The aforementioned board portals—software programs designed to provide directors with secure access to important documents and data and, therefore, increased opportunities for collaboration—rank as both an important opportunity and the kind of thing that can take an entire board down a rabbit hole.

Too much focus on conformity with new technology could inhibit the kind of in-person collaboration and relationship building board directors need to build trust and make informed decisions. Not enough focus on making the director's job easier, more convenient, and surely more secure from a data privacy perspective could leave your board way behind the times.

One curious example of how technology is wagging the dog is the matter of whether your board should consider giving artificial intelligence its own seat on your board. The correct answer, in short, is No!

But the issue of adding some nonhuman form of influence to a board is worth retelling, if only to underline the importance of using good judgment as a director. You should not be fooled into thinking something that sounds chic, interesting, and/or timely but which, upon the application of effective due diligence, really only reveals a tool that should remain in the board's toolbox, should take up your valuable time.

The notion of adding artificial intelligence to a board came to light in 2014 when a Hong Kong–based venture capital firm said it formally recognized an algorithm software called VITAL as an equal—even critical—member of its board of directors.[1]

VITAL, which stands for Validating Investment Tool for Advancing Life Sciences, apparently crunches market data in the regenerative medical sector and helps other board directors make better investment decisions.

Sounds like a great tool with a lot of sharp minds behind it. But a tool nonetheless. The notion of populating a board seat with an algorithm apparently works for that particular firm. Its appointment was certainly enough to garner some attention. But beware the focus on individual examples like this as the next big thing in corporate governance. Sometimes a fad or trend or technology has legs and real staying power. Often, it does not.

> **Straight Talk:** If you keep both eyes on what is good for shareholders in the long-term, you will be less susceptible to the kind of hype and costs that increasingly come with new governance technology.

ACHIEVING MORE BOARD DIVERSITY

It is abundantly clear that today's board directors must commit to breaking down the invisible barriers that for so long have carefully and consistently restricted women's and cultural minorities' access to the boardroom.

These barriers are often vestiges of incompetence, shortsightedness, a lack of planning or understanding of how the board nominating process actually works, and, in some cases, pure bias or prolonged socially driven isolation that results in exclusion. Yet it would be a mistake to appoint more women and leaders from underrepresented populations to boards simply for the sake of improving outward appearances.

Your motivations and action on this topic—as a board and as a director—are your compass and a barometer of the quality of your board. If your intentions are true, you will work proactively to ensure that the search for exceptional board director talent is inclusive. Failing to do so will result in it being exclusive.

There is already a body of evidence, now decades old, that demonstrates just how insular the boardroom has been and how a systemic, historical overreliance on where people went to school, the companies they worked in, the roles they held has created a significant barrier to tapping women and minorities, however they are defined.

For too long, directors have approached the board nominating process putting their own sense of comfort at the core. Boards have historically looked for directors who would "fit," who would understand "how we do things here," and who would "play their part."

All of this gave rise to conformist board directors. Today, the leaders boards really need are collegial in spirit but inquiring and, if need be, constructively disruptive in purpose. They understand that stagnation can paralyze a board and prevent it from administering sound governance oversight, almost always without the board even catching on to the fact that it is grounded in the past.

Advocating for diverse board candidate slates should now be part of any director's change agenda. Business growth cannot coexist with a comfortable set of board directors simply going through the motions of familiar governance protocols.

A PATCHWORK OF HUMAN RELATIONSHIPS

Dr. Tory Herring, a Birmingham, Alabama–based organizational psychologist and executive coach whose sudden passing while we were writing this book only cemented our resolve to reflect his considerable knowledge and experience in the boardroom, shared a very simple message that gets to the heart of our straight talk here. It was this:

> **Straight Talk: The most critical dynamics on today's boards—public, private, not-for-profit, or institutional—are the human ones. The social norms among directors are truly the wellspring of stewardship in the boardroom.**

A board's capacity to clarify misunderstandings and, if need be, engage in some form of conflict resolution is a mirror of its effectiveness as a group of individuals. A director's capacity to understand his or her board peers and what motivates them will impart a sense of confidence when it comes time to engage in critical issues. Knowing others more deeply empowers you to open up. That is when the board really begins to tap its true potential.

> **Straight Talk: The strongest fabric of any board is trust among its directors. If you do not have the trust, it does not give you the strength to be resilient and effective in difficult times.**

Dr. Herring, an endearing Southern gentleman who flew helicopters in the Vietnam War with the First Squadron, Ninth Cavalry, First Air Cavalry Division of the United States Army, combined what he knew about teamwork with his natural compassion for others. For more than three decades, Tory advised boards and management teams about the foundational social pillars of leadership and organizational performance.

Tory became a trusted adviser to a host of high-performing companies during that time, and a cherished mentor and friend to one of this book's co-authors. One of his enduring lessons for clients and colleagues alike was the power of empathy, understanding, humility, and courage—lessons he no doubt learned on the battlefield as well as in the boardroom—and which he so generously shared to advance the interests of effective leadership and board governance.

Tory taught us that building the human, social connections is the key to creating trust. The director's challenge is to develop those connections that foster sufficient enough trust so difficult issues can be surfaced fully. If they are not, nothing real can be done about them. You cannot fully deal with the issue, he knew.

It is never going to be easy. It may create greater insights about possibilities and options and give people on the board the strength to get things into the open—because a lack of trust, action, and transparency actually leads to a board's making things worse rather than better.

Particularly for boards of directors, advisory boards, and other governance panels, the earlier they know about looming issues and risks and the stronger their interpersonal bonds, the more they can do to steer around trouble and avoid crises that can spin out of control quickly. It may not be that we can find a solution, but we may be able to minimize the damage.

Sure, that sounds good. But the key is to make sure those interpersonal dynamics do not become insular or inbred.

Yet because the relationships that constitute the board of directors are so often minimized or discounted, directors and the cause of effective board governance are often penalized as a result. If you overlook or underestimate how the social fabric of your board influences its governance agenda, vision, and practices, you will be unable to fully extract the board's potential and realize your own as an individual director.

Executive coach Kevin Arvin, who likewise counted Dr. Herring as a mentor and friend, outlined for us in chapter 1 many of the leadership, courage, and volunteer-minded instincts directors regularly seek to qualify when it comes to recruiting new people and fresh talent and insight to their boards. Not surprisingly, the influence of Doc Herring still today shapes Kevin's view—and our own—of the "soft skills" that boards find highly desirable in director candidates.

Highly Desirable Soft Skills for Today's Board Director Candidates

1. Executive presence—ability to project gravitas, credibility, confidence, poise under pressure, decisiveness

2. Communication skills, including empathic listening (two ears/one mouth mindfulness), thinking/speaking on your feet, appropriate assertiveness, use of clear language, speaking with passion/energy, and the ability to read an audience or situation

3. Related to communication: conciseness—knowing what you want/need to say and doing it concisely

4. Self-awareness, composure, high emotional intelligence

5. Ability to forge connections with people

6. Ability to "stay in the moment"—focused mindfulness on the people and the topic at hand

7. Consistency in behavior/speech/action to inspire trust and confidence

8. Ability to inspire others to dream, learn, do, and become more

These often-discounted "soft skills" can actually make all the difference. Based on Kevin Arvin's experience as an executive and board candidate coach, a start-up entrepreneur and board adviser, each of the above characteristics is enough to qualify any director or would-be director in terms of "fit" with a board.

More importantly, boards and tenured directors would be wise to seek individuals who measure up on each of these soft skills to determine whether or not it even makes sense to prosecute the qualification of the individual's hard skills.

> **Straight Talk: Recruit for the soft skills first. Establish and qualify that new board candidates can play well with others. Look for a positive attitude and uncover candidates' motivations. Then you will be better prepared to decide how candidates' hard skills compare and how they would upgrade your board's capability.**

Before you can have a board that is high functioning, Dr. Herring believed, you must have individual board members who are high functioning as individuals.

The leaders boards need now—and well into the future—are highly effective contributors, collaborators, and challengers of the status quo.

Directors must ask "Why?" on a regular basis to determine alignment with corporate strategy and the key drivers of organizational investments. Then they must ask "Why?" again, building it into the regular discourse of the board.

Particularly when it comes to evaluating potential new additions to your board, it is best to invest time understanding candidates' natural inclinations for problem solving, their willingness to get to know other board members, and their view of diversity.

It is the diversity of perspectives, experience, knowledge, and skills reflected across the board—and embodied uniquely in each of its members—that provides the breadth and depth required to stand tall in the face of looming business challenges and emerging governance risks.

"When they get up there in the rarified air of the boardroom, most board members—because they have accomplished so much—they are not going to be as willing to discuss their own reservations or lack of understanding of a critical business issue. It is taking a big risk for them," Dr. Herring shared, and so, most often, they will sit and watch at a time when their constituent shareholders desperately need them to lead.

Think about how smart the people on boards are, Dr. Herring asked. "Imagine what they could achieve if they had a full understanding of each other so they could all mutually agree on what do we want to accomplish, how are we going to operate so they could open up enough to one another so each clarified that misunderstanding and broach those topics that are sometimes unapproachable," Tory offered.

"In most social settings, people are a little reluctant. One, they do not want to put themselves at risk. Two, they do not want to embarrass others. Sometimes [that] can be more prominent than the desire or impetus to really tackle what is most important to the company. Sometimes it is those hidden things or the misunderstandings that restrain people. They are not as willing to share as they might be," he added.

"The team role and team dynamic that results when directors increase their knowledge and understanding of each other actually minimizes the reluctance to talk about themselves and ask others about themselves," Dr. Herring shared.

"It is only when those personal relationships develop can you really realize the full potential of a board. It is the ability to understand each other well enough where you can exchange pieces of information that are critical to trust and respect. People are reluctant to share for fear they will tread on some unwritten rule or embarrass themselves, yet it is extraordinarily crucial to good board governance," he added.

The story is that we only get the most from boards or teams when we are able to have those open exchanges that build on the ideas of all members. "That is when we are magnifying things. That is where synergy among board directors creates a 1 + 1 = 3 dynamic," Doc Herring observed.

Why are open exchanges between and among directors so important? Because there are barriers standing in the way.

One of the biggest and most common is this: directors who are too proud and know too much to learn what they need to learn to effectively serve the board.

Then comes the myopia of groupthink. Far too often, directors see things as they want them to be rather than how they really are. Board dynamics are typically painted with far too optimistic or positive and inclusive a lens. Directors tend to be less candid in their assessment of the mutual understanding between board members and the shared understanding across the board.

"If we look at our baseball swing—it is much more perfect in our mind's eye than if we take a projector out there, get some film, and then really evaluate it," Dr. Herring shared. "So, too, are most boards' own self-evaluation scores."

Yet there are also indicators of a truly engaged, high-functioning board. One of them is what Dr. Herring described as consultative leadership. "It is sort of mutually and openly engaging everyone on topics. No one is better than anyone. And so, it is an environment where they work together and get more from working collectively than they would from any one member," he shared.

Culture is the dynamic pathway for the best boards of directors. "How do we establish what is possible? How do we mutually commit to what is possible? When you can establish the ideal among everyone, it makes talking about the actual much simpler and less threatening because, if directors have a good shared picture of the ideal condition, it increases their motivation to get there," Dr. Herring observed. "Today's shortcomings become less threatening. The pursuit of the ideal becomes the next logical step to take versus this giant thing that needs to get accomplished."

When leaders in any management or board role engage with one another about what is possible, it is like a strong tailwind. It pulls people along. They get a clearer vision rather than being entwined in what is currently going on and how that is robbing power from them. Tory

Herring would want you, as a first-time or veteran board director, to create that tailwind.

How? By exhibiting courage, a commitment to learn, humility, and, of course, a desire to engage in the kind of straight talk that gets to the core of key business and governance challenges.

Further, we achieve the leadership and cultural conditions to thrive as boards and directors by inspiring others to similarly reach for their potential while staying grounded in their values.

That is, after all, what this book has truly been all about. We hope it serves you well on your own journey to the boardroom, or in the experience and insights you are already gaining there.

Appendix I

Navigating the Morass of Corporate Jargon: Don't Choke on Alphabet Soup (A Glossary)

In mid-2001, I was in my fifth year as chancellor of the Texas Tech University System. Academia was hard work and a 24/7 commitment, I found, but it can also be a truly rewarding calling.

Since I was perhaps the first nontraditional chancellor in Texas higher education, I was, to say the least, "driven," particularly having come from spending 14 years in the Texas Senate.

I tried to congratulate each graduate personally and, at times, my hand was crushed and crackled in the course of congratulating literally hundreds, even thousands of graduates in any one Texas Tech commencement ceremony.

It was against this backdrop, in early June 2001, when I received a call from Ed Whitacre—then chair and CEO of SBC—asking my wife and me to meet him and his wife at their central Texas ranch for the weekend. Since Ed had been the chair of the board that hired me at Texas Tech, I was looking forward to a weekend enjoying the ranch and getting reconnected with Ed. It turned out to be a career-changing weekend and marked an important and pivotal time in my careers.

We arrived on a Saturday and dialed in from a service gate marked with a huge "W." After exchanging pleasantries and enjoying a nice lunch, Ed and I retreated to the den for what I thought was a friendly invitation to watch some sports event.

Much to my surprise, I was greeted with an offer. "I want you to consider coming to work for us at SBC," Ed said.

I was a bit startled. Yet he went on. "I've got to have major help in governmental affairs," I recall Ed as saying. "We have been getting kicked around in several states."

He then said, "I'd pay you [X] dollars."

To this, I replied, "Ed, I don't know anything about telephones except which end to talk into, and besides, as you know, I'm making a lot more than that as chancellor of Tech each year."

Ed replied, "Well, we can teach you all you need to know about telecommunications. And I'm talking monthly."

A split second in my life moved in slow motion as I tried to comprehend the magnitude of what I had just heard, but to put it mildly and to say I was stunned is an understatement. Without giving it a second thought I blurted out, "Where do I sign?" That's how I became president of external affairs for Southwestern Bell and Southern New England Telephone Company.

In spite of my initial euphoria, however, what I totally underestimated was the reality that telecommunications—just like aviation, finance, law, military, energy, electronics, Internet technology, and numerous other global industries—had evolved its own language, replete with its own alphabet-eating acronyms and other commonly used, insider business terms that help people in a variety of roles communicate more efficiently. Note, please, that I didn't say they help industry insiders communicate more effectively.

The use of these tongue-twisting acronyms and common business phrases was an everyday facet of life in the telecommunications industry at that time. I was bombarded with acronyms such as UNE, UNEP, DSLAM, LEC, ILEC, and CLECs and on and on. In retrospect, I think it would have been easier to learn Russian.

I will never forget my first conference call, shortly after joining SBC, in September 2001. I was thumbing through *Newton's Telecommunications Dictionary*, which is a couple of inches thick and defines thousands of acronyms, looking for virtually every other word.

What a learning curve I had to overcome in those early days of my tenure with the company. Most of the SBC executives and employees around me had 15–20 years' experience in the telecom industry, so I was, at least for the first few weeks, operating at a severe disadvantage.

This is an important observation considering the fact that any leader brought into a corporate role or board seat is indeed under the microscope during his or her early days.

New colleagues, subordinates, and peers want to determine whether you're up to the task, whether you are someone they can respect and follow, and whether you're going to last long or not. To earn their support, the new leader must engender their trust, connect with them personally and with some empathy, and also speak to them in their own industry parlance.

At a recent business meeting in London, one experienced business executive underscored the need for any executive entering a new role (particularly in a new organization) to immerse himself or herself immediately in the unique language of the company and the industry and markets it operates in.

"They really need a dictionary to learn the company's unique vocabulary," the individual observed to my especially well-traveled co-author. Those who cannot immediately lose credibility as well as the opportunity to make a great first impression with new colleagues, subordinates, and other stakeholders.

If you can't talk a good game and do so with some measure of the confidence of people who know the industry better than you, your days in a new job and/or new industry may be numbered.

The reason I share this story about my own early SBC days and the hours I spent with that industry dictionary is because time and time again, board members who have not grown up in a certain industry find they have no clue about what management is saying when board presentations are replete with acronyms and commonly used business phrases.

I have seen and heard this happen time and time again. I would lean over to a fellow board member and ask, "Do you know what 'XYZ' means?" If I get more than one "No" back in reply, I realize I am not the only one in the room who is uninformed and at risk of being overexposed if someone does not interrupt to clarify things.

Let's face it. The reason directors these days will not interrupt is because they do not want to demonstrate that they are ignorant of what some acronym means. To do so might feel embarrassing. But it is your duty, lest you feel that you're gagging on alphabet soup.

One of your primary responsibilities as a director is to *assume nothing*.

Well, here is how to digest the alphabet soup you might be spoon-fed from company management. On one board, I actually got in the habit of challenging every single industry acronym by stopping the presenter and saying, "Acronym Police! Please tell the board what 'XYZ' means."

As a result, amazing changes occurred. Now, in the board books for this company—which for most corporate boards today are generally posted online ahead of each meeting—there is a glossary of acronyms. For the slides and presentations, each acronym is defined every time one is used.

I guarantee this practice will make a hero out of you with the other directors (and even some in management). It is the best way to crack the code, and it is not getting any simpler with the Internet and social media, which is home to some of the newest languages in the world.

Heck, you may find you need a dictionary to understand the text message your grandchild just sent you.

In this appendix we are defining, for your benefit, 100 of the most common acronyms in American business today. The list could easily be extended to 1,000, but these 100 will be a healthy starting point.

For the record, most of the time when sitting near management, I would ask them if they themselves knew what XYZ meant and, in my experience, they wouldn't know the acronym about half the time.

How can you be effective as a director if you do not fully understand management presentations? Does it not make sense to ensure every step of the way that you know what's going on? Otherwise, you are not doing an effective job as a director and you are wasting valuable time at corporate board meetings.

Nodding your head in agreement with all the governance-speak you hear in today's corporate boardrooms can land you and your fellow directors in the hot seat fast.

It is always best to halt a presentation and pause for a translation in the boardroom when some lawyer, accountant, or consultant starts tossing around acronyms and other business terms that begin to sound like a foreign language—even if he or she wants to assume you know exactly what they are telling you. Otherwise, the conversation can spiral out of control without your knowledge.

Policing acronyms as well as commonly used business terms is absolutely your business and responsibility as a director. No one will do this for you unless you require it every time.

In summary, do not be a bit reluctant to assert yourself as the self-appointed Acronym Police Director on the board(s) you serve. Trust me, you will not regret it.

A GLOSSARY OF GOVERNANCE ACRONYMS EVERY DIRECTOR AND WOULD-BE DIRECTOR MUST KNOW

8-K – The "current report" public companies must file with the United States Securities and Exchange Commission to report certain material corporate events that shareholders should know about.

10-K – The annual report required of public traded companies within 60, 75, or 90 days after a business's fiscal year (depending on the category of the filer), providing a comprehensive overview of the company's business and financial condition including audited financial statements. Also known as Form 10-K or 10-K. Although similarly named, the 10-K is different from the company's Annual Report to Shareholders (see below).

10-Q – A quarterly report intended to inform investors about a public company's performance, typically comparing financial performance (typically unaudited) in the last reported quarter to the current quarter, or last year's quarter to this year's quarter. Information for the final quarter of a public company's fiscal year is included in the 10-K, so only three 10-Q filings are made each year. Also known as Form 10-Q or 10-Q, it must be filed as required by the United States Securities and Exchange Commission within 40 or 45 days after the end of the fiscal quarter depending on qualifying SEC regulations.

ABC – Activity-Based Costing

ASC – Accounting Standards Codification

ASP – Application Service Provider

B2B – Business to Business

B2C – Business to Consumer

BFY – Budget Fiscal Year

BIP – Basis Point, shorthand for .01

CAGR – Compound Annual Growth Rate

CAP – Compensation Actually Paid

CEO – Chief Executive Officer

CFO – Chief Financial Officer

CFTC – Commodities Futures Trading Commission

CG – Corporate Governance

CHRO – Chief Human Resources Officer

CIO – Chief Information Officer

CLO – Chief Legal Officer (also GC or General Counsel)

CMO – Chief Marketing Officer

COE – Center of Excellence

COO – Chief Operating Officer

CPI – Consumer Price Index

CRM – Customer Relationship Management

CSP – Commerce Service Provider (typically in e-commerce)

CTO – Chief Technology Officer

D&O – Director's and Officer's (liability insurance)

DB – Defined Benefit (as in a retirement plan)

DES – Data Encryption Standard (typically related to e-commerce)

DJIA – Dow Jones Industrial Average

EAP – Employee Assistance Program

EBITDA – Earnings Before Interest, Taxes, Depreciation, and Amortization

ECB – European Central Bank

EDI – Electronic Data Interchange, a data standard or group of standards that enables two or more computer applications to recognize and understand an electronically transmitted document

EFT – Electronic Funds Transfer

EMEA – Europe, Middle East, and Africa

EPS – Earnings Per Share

ERP – Enterprise Resources Planning

ESOP – Employee Stock Ownership Plan

ETA – Estimated Time of Arrival

ETF – Exchange-Traded Fund

FASB – Financial Accounting Standards Board

FBMS – Financial and Business Management System

FCPA – Foreign Corrupt Practices Act

FDIC – Federal Deposit Insurance Corporation

FTE – Full-Time Employee(s)

FY – Fiscal Year

GAAP – Generally Accepted Accounting Principles

GC – General Counsel (also Chief Legal Officer)

GDP – Gross Domestic Product

GNP – Gross National Product

IPO – Initial Public Offering

ISS – Institutional Shareholder Services, Inc.

KPI – Key Performance Indicator(s)

LIBOR (also Libor) – London Interbank Offered Rate

LLC – Limited Liability Corporation

LLP – Limited Liability Partnership

MD&A – Management Discussion and Analysis

MSRP – Manufacturer's Suggested Retail Price

NACD – National Association of Corporate Directors

NASDAQ – National Association of Securities Dealers Automated Quotation

NAV – Net Asset Value

NDA – Non-Disclosure Agreement

NLRB – National Labor Relations Board

Non-GAAP – Earnings measures that may include cash earnings, EBITDA, pro-forma income, and operating earnings and which fall outside the definition of Generally Accepted Accounting Principles. Many companies report non-GAAP earnings in addition to the required GAAP earnings.

NOPAT – Net Operating Profit After Tax

NPV – Net Present Value

NYSE – New York Stock Exchange

OEM – Original Equipment Manufacturer

OTC – Over The Counter

P&L – Profit and Loss (also called an Income Statement, a Statement of Profit and Loss, or an Income and Expense Statement). A statement reflecting the revenue, costs, and expenses realized by a business entity during a specified period of time, usually a fiscal quarter or fiscal year.

PCAOB – Public Company Accounting Oversight Board

PE – Price to Earnings (ratio) or Private Equity

POS – Point of Sale

PSP – Profit-Sharing Plan

Q1, Q2, Q3, Q4 – First Quarter (either of a calendar or a company's fiscal year), Second Quarter, Third Quarter, Fourth Quarter

QA, QC – Quality Assurance, Quality Control

RACI Chart – A system for assigning roles and responsibilities in a group pursuit of desired outcomes. R is for Responsible, A is for Accountable, C is for needs to be Consulted, and I is for needs to be Informed.

Real GDP – Gross Domestic Product adjusted for changes in prices

REIT – Real Estate Investment Trust

RFP – Request For Proposal

ROE – Return On Equity

ROI – Return On Investment

ROIC – Return On Invested Capital

ROS – Return On Sales

S&P – Standard & Poor's

SAAS – Software As A Service

SEC – United States Securities and Exchange Commission

SME – Small to Medium-size Enterprise or Subject Matter Expert

SSL – Secure Sockets Layer is a widely used protocol for encrypting data that permits the secure transmission of credit card transactions from point of sale to the card issuer's systems.

SWOT Analysis – An analysis of a company's Strengths, Weaknesses, Opportunities, and Threats

T&E – Travel and Entertainment, Travel and Expenses, Time and Effort, Time and Expense, Trade and Exchange

TCO – Total Cost of Ownership

TQM – Total Quality Management

TSA – Tax-Sheltered Annuity or United States Transportation Security Administration

TSR – Total Shareholder Return

TTP – Trusted Third Party

URL – Uniform Resource Locator, a full website address such as http://www.southwest.com

USP – Unique Selling Point

VAT – Value-Added Tax

VC – Venture Capital

BONUS GLOSSARY OF COMMONLY USED BUSINESS TERMS

Annual Report to Shareholders – A report to the shareholders of public companies distributed before its annual meeting to elect directors.

Balance Sheet – A financial statement or "snapshot" summarizing a company's assets, liabilities, and shareholders' equity through the end of a specified date, such as the end of its financial year. This document helps investors and other interested parties understand what the company owns (assets), what it owes (liabilities), and ownership equity. Also known as the Statement of Financial Position.

Cautionary Forward-Looking Statements – Statements by the management of public companies including predictions about future business conditions subject to a disclaimer required by the United States Securities and Exchange Commission and intended to remind investors that what is disclosed may be speculation. In the United States, the Private Securities Litigation Reform Act of 1995 provides certain safe harbor provisions against fraud claims dealing with forward-looking statements that may include words such as "believes," "projects," "will," and "plans," recognizing that shareholders often ask company management about what may happen in the business in the future and that while management is often in a position to see trends, it cannot predict what will come to pass.

Data Mining – The process of using sophisticated software and techniques to identify commercially relevant statistical patterns or relationships in online databases and related files.

Death by Committee – Any tactic of diversion or evasion meant to obstruct the serious, meaningful consideration of a proposal by assigning a committee to review it.

Defalcation – An amount of money misappropriated by an individual charged and trusted with its custody and proper management, or the act related thereto.

e-Commerce – The exchange of goods, information products, or services via an electronic medium such as the Internet.

Form 8-K – Defined by the SEC as the "current report" companies are required to file for the purpose of disclosing information that shareholders should know about.

Garbatrage[1] – Unwarranted market movement and volume based on merger rumors.

Investigative Due Diligence – The gathering of intelligence, for example, on corporate transactions such as mergers or new business relationships, to help the board make informed decisions aimed at reducing enterprise risks.

Material Misstatement – An accidental or intentional misstatement that may be included in a company's publicly released financial records that may influence a company's value and/or stock price, which may also affect the economic decision making of individuals using or relying on those financial statements.

On Boarding – A process through which a management employee or senior executive leader receives consensus stakeholder feedback about his or her early impact in a new role and/or with a new employer so they have a sense of perceptions of their performance, typically within their first year on the job.

Reg FD – Regulation Fair Disclosure was adopted by the United States Securities and Exchange Commission to address the selective disclosure of information by publicly traded companies and other issuers. It provides that when an issuer discloses material nonpublic information to certain individuals or entities, the issuer must make public disclosure of that information with the intent of promoting full and fair disclosure.

Regulation S-K – The United States Securities Act of 1933 prescribed the reporting requirements for various filings with the Securities and Exchange Commission used by public companies. Companies are also often referred to as issuers (issuing or considering the issue of shares to the public), filers (entities that must file reports with the SEC), and registrants (entities that must register with the SEC).

Spoof or Spoofing[2] – Offers or bids that do not represent a genuine offer to trade stocks and are withdrawn if interest is shown.

Uncorrected Misstatements[3] – Related to the release and distribution of financial statements that are not, in fact, supported by an organization's actual financial performance or standing, these often surface in the course of audits and are the subject of FASB guidance, as well as being serious business for the board.

Sample Balance Sheet

ABC Corporation
Sample Balance Sheet
as of
December 31, 2015

	in thousands December 31, 2015	*in thousands* December 31, 2014
Assets	**2015**	**2014**
Current Assets		
Cash & Cash Equivalents	39,000	39,000
Accounts Receivable	900,000	820,000
Inventory	145,000	141,000
Prepaid Expenses	45,000	40,000
Short-Term Investments	30,000	25,000
Total Current Assets	1,159,000	1,065,000
Fixed (Long-Term) Assets		
Long-Term Investments	30,000	80,000
Property, Plant, and Equipment	11,300,000	10,500,000
Less: Allowance for Depreciation & Amortization	250,000	225,000
Total Fixed Assets	11,580,000	10,805,000

Other Assets		
Goodwill	1,500,000	1,500,000
Other Assets	2,300,000	2,400,000
Total Other Assets	3,800,000	3,900,000
Total Assets	**16,539,000**	**15,770,000**
Liabilities and Shareholders' Equity		
Current Liabilities		
Accounts Payable	600,000	580,000
Accrued Liabilities	40,000	35,000
Short/Current Long-Term Debt	1,500,000	1,300,000
Other Current Liabilities	290,000	305,000
Total Current Liabilities	2,430,000	2,220,000
Long-Term Liabilities		
Long-Term Debt	7,900,000	7,750,000
Other Liabilities	990,000	1,000,000
Total Long-Term Liabilities	8,890,000	8,750,000
Shareholders' Equity		
Common Stock	2,200,000	2,200,000
Preferred Stock	40,500	40,500
*Retained Earnings	2,978,500	2,559,500
Total Shareholders' Equity	5,219,000	4,800,000
Total Liabilities and Shareholders' Equity	**16,539,000**	**15,770,000**

*Moneys retained by Company to be reinvested in core business, pay debt, and not distributed to shareholders.

Board and Committee Self-Evaluation Form

As required by the governance standards of the New York Stock Exchange (the "NYSE"), the following questions are designed to gather director input on the company board's performance and effectiveness, including the performance and effectiveness of its committees.

In accordance with the NYSE's Rules and the charter of the Nominating and Corporate Governance Committee (NCG), the NCG is responsible for overseeing an evaluation at least annually of the performance of the board and the board's committees and reporting its conclusions to the full board.

As stated in the company's Corporate Governance Guidelines, the purpose of the self-evaluation is to improve board and committee performance generally and not to target the performance of individual directors. The NCG may use the results of its evaluation in determining the criteria for directors to be considered to fill any vacancies on the board or on its committees and for inclusion in the slate of directors to be recommended by the board at the Annual Meeting of Shareholders. If there is insufficient space for your answers, attach additional sheets as needed.

BOARD STRUCTURE

1. Does the board as a whole possess the right skills and background for the current issues facing the company?

    ☐ Yes   ☐ No   ☐ Neutral

    Comments: _____

    _____

    _____

    _____

2. Does the board have the right number of directors?

    ☐ Yes   ☐ No   ☐ Neutral

    Comments: _____

    _____

    _____

    _____

3. Are you satisfied with the process for selecting directors?

    ☐ Yes   ☐ No   ☐ Neutral

    Comments: _____

    _____

    _____

    _____

KEY BOARD RESPONSIBILITIES

1. Some key elements that facilitate the board's ability to effectively carry out its responsibilities are:

    a. Knowledge of the company's strategic plan, operations, mission, culture, and vision

    b. Knowledge of the company's culture and core values

    c. Familiarity with organized labor and labor issues

    d. Knowledge of the technical and economic aspects of the company's industry

    e. Insights into new technological trends and developments

    f. The ability to understand and use the company's financial data

    g. Familiarity with corporate law and tax matters

    h. Familiarity with financing matters

    i. Familiarity with worldwide, U.S., and state and local politics and governmental affairs

How effective is the board overall in bringing together these key elements?

Not Effective   Effective   Very Effective

What additional information, presentations, or other steps would you like to see from management to assist the board with strengthening any of these elements?

_____

_____

_____

_____

2. How effective is the company's strategic planning process, including board member opportunity to have input into the strategic plan?

Not Effective   Effective   Very Effective

Do you have any comments, suggestions, or specific changes you would recommend?

_____

_____

_____

_____

3. How satisfied are you with management's ongoing communications to the board?

Dissatisfied   Satisfied   Very Satisfied

Do you have any comments, suggestions, or specific changes you would recommend?

_____

_____

_____

_____

4. Are there any corporate governance areas you would like the board or any of its committees to address in more detail?

    ☐ Yes   ☐ No

    What are they?

    _____

    _____

    _____

    _____

5. How effective is the current succession planning process?

    |_____|_____|_____|
         Not Effective   Effective   Very Effective

    Comments: _____

    _____

    _____

    _____

6. How effective is the CEO evaluation process?

    |_____|_____|_____|
         Not Effective   Effective   Very Effective

    Comments: _____

    _____

    _____

    _____

7. Are you satisfied with your contacts with management outside of board meetings and with your opportunities to meet and observe potential successors to key management positions?

    ☐ Yes   ☐ No   ☐ Neutral

    Comments: _____

    _____

    _____

8. How effective is the current process for developing, reviewing, and issuing the Annual Report on Form 10-K, Proxy Statement, quarterly earnings releases, and Forms 10-Q?

|_____|_____|_____|
Not Effective   Effective   Very Effective

Do you have any suggestions?

_____

_____

_____

_____

9. Are you satisfied with the current Annual Meeting of Shareholders format?

☐ Yes   ☐ No   ☐ Neutral

Do you have any suggestions?

_____

_____

_____

_____

BOARD MEETINGS

1. The board has six regularly scheduled meetings per year. Do you favor maintaining the current board meeting schedule?

☐ Yes   ☐ No   ☐ Neutral

Comments: _____

_____

_____

_____

2. How satisfied are you with the current board agendas?

|_____|_____|_____|
Dissatisfied   Satisfied   Very Satisfied

Do you have any suggestions on additional subjects you would like covered or materials or information you would like provided?

_____

_____

_____

_____

3. How satisfied are you with the advance information you receive before board meetings?

    |_____|_____|_____|
         Dissatisfied   Satisfied   Very Satisfied

    What else would you like?

    _____

    _____

    _____

    _____

4. How satisfied are you with the current handling of meeting and travel logistics, payment of expenses and fees, and overall administrative matters?

    |_____|_____|_____|
         Dissatisfied   Satisfied   Very Satisfied

    Do you have any suggestions for improvements?

    _____

    _____

    _____

    _____

5. How effective are the board's executive sessions?

    |_____|_____|_____|
         Not Effective   Effective   Very Effective

    Comments: _____

    _____

    _____

    _____

BOARD COMMITTEE STRUCTURE AND PERFORMANCE

1. The board has established five standing board committees: Audit (required), Compensation (required), Nominating and Corporate Governance (required), Safety and Compliance Oversight, and Executive. How effective are the current committee structures, rotation of members and chairs, and operating procedures?

    |_____|_____|_____|
         Not Effective   Effective   Very Effective

Do you have any suggestions you would like the board or any particular committee to address?

_____

_____

_____

_____

2. How satisfied are you with the way committee agendas are prepared and circulated?

| |_____|_____|_____| |
Dissatisfied   Satisfied   Very Satisfied

Do you have any related suggestions or requests with respect to any of the committees?

_____

_____

_____

_____

3. Do you have any suggestions for any of the committees on which you serve regarding (a) subjects that should receive more or less committee focus, (b) materials provided, or (c) presentations and discussion?

_____

_____

_____

_____

4. How satisfied are you with the way information and logistical support are provided to the committees?

| |_____|_____|_____| |
Dissatisfied   Satisfied   Very Satisfied

Do you have any related suggestions or requests with respect to any of the committees?

_____

_____

_____

_____

5. Is the communication and coordination among the committees adequate?

    ☐ Yes   ☐ No   ☐ Neutral

    Comments: _____

    _____

    _____

    _____

6. Do you have any suggestions for any of the committees on which you serve
    regarding scheduling?

    ☐ Yes   ☐ No

    Comments: _____

    _____

    _____

    _____

7. How effective was the Audit Committee in performing its responsibilities,
    as outlined in its charter?

    |_____|_____|_____|
        Not Effective   Effective   Very Effective

    Comments: _____

    _____

    _____

    _____

8. How effective was the Compensation Committee in performing its respon-
    sibilities, as outlined in its charter?

    |_____|_____|_____|
        Not Effective   Effective   Very Effective

    Comments: _____

    _____

    _____

    _____

9. How effective was the Nominating and Corporate Governance Committee in performing its responsibilities, as outlined in its charter?

Not Effective	Effective	Very Effective

Comments: _____

_____

_____

10. How effective was the Safety and Compliance Oversight Committee in performing its responsibilities, as outlined in its charter?

Not Effective	Effective	Very Effective

Comments: _____

_____

_____

_____

11. How effective was the Executive Committee in performing its responsibilities, as outlined in its charter?

Not Effective	Effective	Very Effective

Comments: _____

_____

_____

_____

ADDITIONAL QUESTIONS FOR AUDIT COMMITTEE MEMBERS

1. Does the Audit Committee have a positive working relationship with management, the internal auditors, and the independent auditors?

    ☐ Yes   ☐ No   ☐ Not sure

    Comments: _____

    _____

    _____

2. Does the Audit Committee challenge management, the internal auditors, and the independent auditors with its own view on issues?

    ☐ Yes   ☐ No   ☐ Not sure

    Comments: _____

    _____

    _____

3. Are differences of opinion on issues resolved to the satisfaction of the Audit Committee?

    ☐ Yes   ☐ No   ☐ Not sure

    Comments: _____

    _____

    _____

4. Is the Audit Committee Charter used as a document to guide the Audit Committee in its efforts and to help guide its agenda?

    ☐ Yes   ☐ No   ☐ Not sure

    Comments: _____

    _____

    _____

5. Are the members of the Audit Committee financially literate?

    ☐ Yes   ☐ No   ☐ Not sure

    Comments: _____

    _____

    _____

6. Are appropriate internal and external support and resources available to the Audit Committee?

    ☐ Yes   ☐ No   ☐ Not sure

    Comments: _____

    _____

    _____

7. Are the company's financial reporting processes stronger as a result of management's interaction with the Audit Committee?

    ☐ Yes   ☐ No   ☐ Not sure

    Comments: _____

    _____

    _____

8. Is the Audit Committee cognizant of the line between oversight and management and does it endeavor to respect that line?

☐ Yes ☐ No ☐ Not sure

Comments: _____

_____

_____

9. Does the Audit Committee conduct executive sessions in a manner that offers a "safe haven" to the individual, while at the same time asking tough and necessary questions, evaluating the answers, and pursuing issues that might arise to a satisfactory resolution?

☐ Yes ☐ No ☐ Not sure

Comments: _____

_____

_____

10. Do Audit Committee members participate in some form of continuing education to stay abreast of changes in the financial accounting and reporting, regulatory, and ethics areas?

☐ Yes ☐ No ☐ Not sure

Comments: _____

_____

_____

11. Does the Audit Committee do its part to ensure the objectivity of the internal audit team?

☐ Yes ☐ No ☐ Not sure

Comments: _____

_____

_____

12. Does the Audit Committee Charter clearly set forth the nature and scope of the Audit Committee's responsibilities?

☐ Yes ☐ No ☐ Not sure

Comments: _____

_____

_____

13. Do Audit Committee meetings occur often enough and are they effective and of an appropriate length to allow discussion of relevant issues consistent with the committee's responsibilities?

☐ Yes   ☐ No   ☐ Not sure

Comments: _____

_____

_____

14. Does the Audit Committee demonstrate its direct responsibility for the appointment, compensation, and oversight of the work of the independent auditor?

☐ Yes   ☐ No   ☐ Not sure

Comments: _____

_____

_____

15. Does the Audit Committee oversee changes in internal audit leadership?

☐ Yes   ☐ No   ☐ Not sure

Comments: _____

_____

_____

GENERAL COMMENTS

1. Please comment on any other areas you feel need improvement or that have not been covered by this assessment tool.

_____

_____

_____

_____

2. Are there any topics not covered in this questionnaire that you feel should be addressed to evaluate the performance of the board and its committees?

_____

_____

_____

_____

Notes

CHAPTER 1: HOW TO GET APPOINTED TO A BOARD WHEN YOU'RE NOT A HOUSEHOLD NAME: BRING SOMETHING THE BOARD WANTS BUT DOESN'T HAVE

1. Nathan Bomey, "Billionaire Says She Will Join Diet Company's Board of Directors, and Oprah's 10% Stake Sends Weight Watchers Stock Soaring," *USA Today*, October 20, 2015.

CHAPTER 2: PUTTING SHAREHOLDERS FIRST . . . NOT LAST: THE CASE FOR DIVIDENDS AND THE ROLE OF INDEPENDENT DIRECTORS

An excellent summary and checklist for board governance requirements was prepared by the law firm of Weil, Gotshal & Manges, LLP, can be found online at: http://www.weil.com/~/media/files/pdfs/150154_pcag_board_requirements_chart_2015_v21.pdf. This summary and the checklist were used extensively in chapters 2, 5, and 8. Excerpts from this article are reprinted by permission of the firm of Weil, Gotshal & Manges, LLP. It is highly recommended that directors of publicly traded companies use checklists such as this for informed compliance.

1. Requirement for Public Company Boards: Weil, Gotshal & Manges LLP Public Company Advisory Group; March 2015; http://www.weil.com/~/media/files/pdfs/150154_pcag_board_requirements_chart_2015_v21.pdf (p. 1).

2. Section 303A.01, NYSE Listed Company Manual; Rule 5605 (b)(1), NASDAQ Listing Rules; Weil, *supra* (p. 2).

3. Section 303A.03, NYSE Listed Company Manual; Rule 5605 (b)(2), NASDAQ Listing Rules.

4. Sections 303A.06, 303A.07, 303A.05, 303A.04, NYSE Listed Company Manual.

5. Rules 5605(c), 5605(d)(2), 5605(a)(2), 5605(e), NASDAQ Listing Rules.

6. SOX Section 407; SEC Regulation, S-K Item 407(a)(5); Section 303A.07(a), NYSE Listed Company Manual.

7. Section 303A.06, NYSE Listed Company Manual; Rule 5605 (c)(3), NASDAQ Listing Rules.

8. Section 303A.05, NYSE Listed Company Commentary; Rules 5605 (d)(1), 5605 (d)(6), NASDAQ Listing Rules.

9. Section 303A.02(a)(ii), Section 303A(2)(a) NYSE Listed Company Manual; Rule 5605(d)(2)(A), 5605(d)(6), NASDAQ Listing Rules; NASDAQ IM-5605-6.

10. Section 303A.02(a)(ii), NYSE Listed Company Manual; NASDAQ IM-5605-6; Rule 5605(d)(2)(A), NASDAQ Listing Rules. Also see SEC Regulation S-K, Item 407(e)(iii).

11. SEC Regulation S-K, Item 407 (e)(5); Commentary to Section 303A.05, NYSE Listed Company Manual; Rules 5605 (d)(1), 5605 (d)(6), NASDAQ Listing Rules.

12. Section 303A.05(6)(iii), NYSE Listed Company Manual; Weil, supra at p. 11.

13. SEC Regulation S-K, Item 407(e)(2); Section 303A.05, NYSE Listed Company Manual.

14. Section 303A.05(6); Commentary to NYSE Listed Company Manual.

15. SEC Regulation S-K.

16. Section 303 A.04 (a), NYSE Listed Company Manual; Rule 5605 (e), NASDAQ Listing Rules.

17. Sections 303A.04, 303A.05(e), NYSE Listed Company Manual.

18. Section 303A.04, Commentary, NYSE Listed Company Manual.

19. SEC Regulation S-K, Item 407 (c)(2)(i).

20. Sections 723 (b) and 763 (a), Dodd-Frank.

21. Section 165, Dodd-Frank.

22. Section 406, Sarbanes-Oxley (SOX 406).

23. SEC Regulation S-K, Item 406.

24. SEC Regulation S-K, Item 406 (c).

25. SOX Section 406; Section 303A.10, NYSE Listed Company Manual.

26. Section 303A.10, NYSE Listed Company Manual; SOX Section 406.

27. Section 303A.10, SEC Regulation S-K, Item 406 (c).

28. Section 303A.09, NYSE Listed Company Manual.

29. Section 303A.10, NYSE Listed Company Manual; SEC Regulation S-K Item 406(c).

30. Section 303A.12 (a), NYSE Listed Company Manual.

31. Rule 5625, NASDAQ Listing Rule.

32. Section 303A.12 (c), NYSE Listed Company Manual.

33. Section 303A.13; Chapter 8, NYSE Listed Company Manual; Rules 5250(b)(2), 5810(b); Rules 5805 through 5840, NASDAQ Listing Rules.

34. Scott Stawski, "10 Stocks with High Return on Invested Capital—And Why You Should Care," TheStreet.com, September 8, 2015, http://www.thestreet.com/story/13279076/1/10-stocks-with-high-return-on-invested-capital-and-why-you-should-care.html.

35. Section 703.02 (Part 1), Stock Split/Stock Rights/Stock Dividend Listing Process, nysemanual.nyse.com, NYSE Listed Company Manual.

CHAPTER 3: THE HIDE AND SEEK GAME OF CORPORATE FINANCE: UNDERSTANDING BALANCE SHEETS AND CORPORATE ECONOMICS

1. Federal Accounting Standards Advisory Board, fasab.gov, Authoritative Source of Guidance, Accounting and Other Pronouncements. 2011, http://www.fasab.gov/accounting-standards/authoritative-source-of-gaap/.

2. The Securities Exchange Act of 1934, 10-Q, 10-K, Section 13 or 15 (d).

3. BusinessDictionary.com, Shareholders Equity, http://www.businessdictionary.com/definition/shareholders-equity.html.

4. Investing Answers, Free Cash Flow, http://www.investinganswers.com/financial-dictionary/financial-statement-analysis/free-cash-flow-1000.

5. The Securities Exchange Act of 1934, 10-Q, 10-K, Section 13 or 15 (d).

6. The Securities Exchange Act of 1934, SEC.gov, Form 8-K; Section 13 or 15 (d).

7. U.S. Securities and Exchange Commission, Fair Disclosure, Regulation FD of 1934.

8. SEC Concept Release: International Accounting Standards, 17CFR Parts 230 and 240; Concept Release.

9. *Financial Times*; ft.com/lexicon; Definition of Derivatives, http://lexicon.ft.com/Term?term=derivatives.

CHAPTER 4: WHEN BAD THINGS HAPPEN TO GOOD BOARDS: PROTECTING SHAREHOLDERS AND YOUR REPUTATION

1. Enron Corporation Press Release, February 6, 2001, http://www.propagandacritic.com/articles/examples.enron.html.

2. Peter Elkind, "Enron on Trial," *Fortune*, January 23, 2006, Archival Feature republished May 12, 2013, http://fortune.com/2013/05/12/enron-on-trial-fortune-2006/.

CHAPTER 5: MEETING YOUR FIDUCIARY RESPONSIBILITY: YOUR PERSONAL DECLARATION OF INDEPENDENCE

1. Section 303A.01, NYSE Listed Company Manual; Rule 5605 (b)(1), NASDAQ Listing Rules.

2. Sections 303A.06, 303A.07, 303.05, 303A.04, 303A.05, NYSE Listed Company Manual; Rule 5605 (d)(2), 5605 (d)(2)(A), 5605 (a)(2), NASDAQ Listing Rules.

3. Section 303A.02 (a), NYSE Listed Company Manual; Rule 5605 (a)(2), NASDAQ Listing Rules.

4. *Requirement for Public Company Boards*, Weil, Gotshal & Manges LLP Public Company Advisory Group; March 2015; http://www.weil.com/~/media/files/pdfs/150154_pcag_board_requirements_chart_2015_v21.pdf.

5. Rule 5605 (a)(2), NASDAQ Listing Rules; NASDAQ IM-5605.

6. Rule 5605 (a)(2), NASDAQ Listing Rules; NASDAQ IM-5605; Exchange Act Rule 16a.

7. The Sarbanes-Oxley Act of 2002, SOX Section 301; Exchange Act Rule 10A-3 (b)(1), Exchange Act Rule 10A-3(e)(8), Rule 10A–3(e)(1), Rule 10A-3(b)(1)(iv)B.

8. *Requirement for Public Company Boards*, Weil, Gotshal & Manges LLP Public Company Advisory Group; March 2015; http://www.weil.com/~/media/files/pdfs/150154 pcag board requirements chart 2015 v21.pdf.

9. Section 303A.03, NYSE Listed Company Manual.

10. Rule 5605 (b((2), NASDAQ Listing Rules; NASDAQ IM-5605-2.

11. Section 303A.03, NYSE Listed Company Manual.

12. Section 303A.07 (b) (ii-iii); Section 303A.05(b)(iii), NYSE Listed Company Manual Commentary Requirement for Public Company Boards, Weil, Gotshal & Manges LLP Public Company Advisory Group; March 2015; http://www.weil.com/~/media/files/pdfs/150154_pcag_board_requirements_chart_2015_v21.pdf; NYSE Listed Company Manual, Commentary, Section 303A.05(b) iii.

CHAPTER 7: GETTING CEO SEARCH AND SUCCESSION RIGHT THE FIRST TIME: DON'T FUMBLE THE HANDOFF

1. Brian Leigh, "Mike Leach Says He Might Ask the Janitor for Football Advice," *Bleacher Report*, May 19, 2014, http://bleacherreport.com/articles /2068508-mike-leach-says-he-has-asked-the-janitor-for-football-advice.

CHAPTER 8: THE AUDIT COMMITTEE: THE BOARD'S "FIRE DEPARTMENT"

In addition to the summary and checklist prepared by the law firm of Weil, Gotshal & Manges, LLP, an excellent Audit Committee checklist and compliance timeline by the firm of Gibson, Dunn & Crutcher can be found online at: http://www.gibsondunn.com/publications/Documents/AuditCommitteeCheck list.pdf. For attribution purposes, it was consulted extensively in the writing of chapter 8.

1. Section 303A.07 (a), NYSE Listed Company Manual.

2. The Sarbanes-Oxley Act of 2002, Section 407; SEC Regulation S-K, Item 407 (d)(5).

3. Securities and Exchange Act of 1934 ("Exchange Act") Rule 10A-3, 10A-3 (b)(2); Section 303A.07 (b)(iii), NYSE Listed Company Manual; Rule 5605 (c)(3)(i) NASDAQ Listing Rules.

4. Section 303A.07 (b)(i), NYSE Listed Company Manual.

5. Joann S. Lublin and T. Michael Rapoport, "The Audit Committee—The Board's Fire Department," *Wall Street Journal*, February 3, 2015.

6. Exchange Act, Rule 10A-3 (b), (2), (3), (4), and (5).

7. Section 303A.07 (b)(i), NYSE Listed Company Manual.

8. Section 303A.07 (b)(ii) and (iii), NYSE Listed Company Manual.

9. Securities and Exchange Act of 1934, Rule 10A-3(b), (2), (3), (4), and (5); Rule 5605 (c)(i), NASDAQ Listing Rules.

10. SEC Regulation S-K, Item 407 (d)(1); Section 303A.07 (b), NYSE Listed Company Manual.

11. SEC Regulation S-K, Item 407 (d)(5)(ii).

12. SEC Regulation S-K, Item 407 (d)(5)(iii).

13. Exchange Act, Rule 10A-3.

14. Section 303A.07 (b)(iii)(E), NYSE Listed Company Manual.

15. Section 303A.07 (c), NYSE Listed Company Manual.

16. Section 303A.07 (b)(iii)(c), NYSE Listed Company Manual, Commentary.

17. Section 303A.07 (b)(iii)(b), NYSE Listed Company Manual.

18. Exchange Act, Rule 13 (a)(15c), Item 9a of Form 10-K, Item 408 (a) of Regulation S-K.

19. University of Delaware, Finance, Internal Audit, Internal Control Definition, http://www.udel.edu/Treasurer/intcntrldef.html.

20. Public Company Accounting Oversight Board, pcaobus.org.

21. EY Center for Board Matters, "Financial Restatements: Understanding Differences and Significance," May 2015, http://www.ey.com/Publication /vwLUAssets/EY-financial-restatements-understanding-differences-and -significance/$FILE/EY-financial-restatements-understanding-differences-and -significance-cover.pdf.

22. PCAOB, "An Audit of Internal Control over Financial Reporting That Is Integrated with an Audit of Financial Statements," A-3, pcaobus.org, Auditing Standard No. 5.

23. PCAOB, Auditing Standard No. 5, A-11, pcaobus.org.

24. PCAOB, Auditing Standard No. 5, A-7, pcaobus.org.

25. SEC Form 8-K, Section 302 Sarbanes-Oxley, ey.com, "Financial Restatements: Understanding Differences and Significance," Ernst & Young; Exchange Act Rule 13 a-15 (c).

26. Exchange Act, Section 13 or 15 (d); SEC Regulation FD, 17 CFR 243.100, 243.101.

27. EY Center for Board Matters, "Financial Restatements: Understanding Differences and Significance," May 2015, http://www.ey.com/Publication /vwLUAssets/EY-financial-restatements-understanding-differences-and -significance/$FILE/EY-financial-restatements-understanding-differences-and -significance-cover.pdf.

28. Section 303A.07 (b)(iii)(c), NYSE Listed Company Manual.

29. SEC Regulation S-K Item 601 (6)(31); Sarbanes-Oxley Act of 2002, Section 302; Exchange Act, Rule 13a-15d.

30. Sarbanes-Oxley Act of 2002, Section 406.

31. Securities and Exchange Commission, SEC Regulation S-K, Item 406 (c).

32. Sarbanes-Oxley Act of 2002, Section 806, Regulation 21F; Exchange Act; Dodd-Frank Section 922 (a).

33. Section 303A.07 (b)(iii), NYSE Listed Company Manual.

34. Foreign Corrupt Practices Act of 1977 (FCPA), 15 USC 78dd et. seq.

35. Code of Federal Regulations, 17 CFR 243, 100–243, 103 Fair Disclosure Regulation.

36. Cornell University, School of Law, "Insider Trading, An Overview," Legal Information Institute, October 26, 2015, law.cornell.edu.

37. Joseph Mariano and Brett Arnold, "It's Getting Harder to Put Wall-Streeters Behind Bars," *Business Insider*, businessinsider.com, Finance, October 25, 2015.

CHAPTER 9: THE FANTASYLAND OF EXECUTIVE COMPENSATION: DIRECTORS OUGHT TO KNOW HOW MUCH IS TOO MUCH

1. Matt Krantz, "9 CEOs Paid 800 Times More Than Their Workers," *USA Today*, August 6, 2015, http://www.usatoday.com/story/money/markets /2015/08/05/ceos-paid-many-times-more/31148137/.

2. Matt Krantz, "9 CEOs Paid 800 Times More Than Their Workers," *USA Today*, August 6, 2015, http://www.usatoday.com/story/money/markets /2015/08/05/ceos-paid-many-times-more/31148137/.

3. Gary Strauss, "Target Says Pay for Ousted CEO Too High," *USA Today*, May 19, 2014, http://www.usatoday.com/story/money/business/2014/05/19/target -says-pay-for-former-ceo-was-too-high/9277497/.

4. Gary Strauss, "Restoration Hardware's Restorative CEO Comp: $66 Million," *USA Today*, May 15, 2015, http://www.usatoday.com/story/money /business/2014/05/15/restoration-hardwares-restorative-comp-for-ceo-xxx -million/9141035/.

5. Gary Strauss, "Time Warner Cable Guy Glenn Britt: $118m in 2013 Comp," *USA Today*, April 29, 2014, http://www.usatoday.com/story/money /business/2014/04/29/time-warner-cable-guy-glenn-britt-118m-in-2013 -comp/8478063/.

6. Gary Strauss, "Ex Wal-Mart CEO's Deferred Pay: $140 Million," *USA Today*, April 24, 2014, http://www.usatoday.com/story/money/business /2014/04/23/wal-marts-departed-ceo-had-pension-valued-at-140-million /8061789/.

7. Gary Strauss, "Chesapeake Energy's McClendon Got $53 Million Severance," *USA Today*, April 17, 2014, http://www.usatoday.com/story/money /business/2014/04/17/chesapeake-energys-mcclendon-got-53-million-severance /7840975/.

8. Charles Riley, "Ousted Yahoo Exec Gets $58 Million Golden Parachute," CNN Money, April 17, 2014, http://money.cnn.com/2014/04/17/technology /de-castro-yahoo-pay/.

9. Joe Nocera, Opinion-Editorial, "C.E.O. Pay Goes Up, Up and Away!," *New York Times*, April 14, 2014, http://www.nytimes.com/2014/04/15/opinion /ceo-pay-goes-up-up-and-away.html?_r=0.

10. Securities and Exchange Commission, Press Release 2015-160, "SEC Adopts Rule for Pay Ratio Disclosure," August 5, 2015, http://www.sec.gov /news/pressrelease/2015-160.html.

11. Securities and Exchange Commission, Press Release 2015-160, "SEC Adopts Rule for Pay Ratio Disclosure," August 5, 2015, http://www.sec.gov /news/pressrelease/2015-160.html.

12. Securities and Exchange Commission, Press Release 2015-160, "SEC Adopts Rule for Pay Ratio Disclosure," August 5, 2015, http://www.sec.gov /news/pressrelease/2015-160.html.

CHAPTER 10: CYBERSECURITY IS EVERY DIRECTOR'S BUSINESS: WHY CYBERATTACKS ARE EXISTENTIAL THREATS

1. David Goldman and Jose Pagliery, "The Worst Hacks of All Time," CNN Money, June 5, 2015, http://money.cnn.com/gallery/technology/2015/02 /05/worst-hacks-ever/.

2. "Target Cyberattack by Overseas Hackers May Have Compromised up to 40 Million Cards," December 20, 2013, *Washington Post*, https://www.wash ingtonpost.com/business/economy/target-cyberattack-by-overseas-hackers -may-have-compromised-up-to-40-million-cards/2013/12/20/2c2943cc-69b5 -11e3-a0b9-249bbb34602c_story.html.

3. "Target Part of a Broad Cyber-Attack, Russian Hackers Allegedly Involved," RT.com, January 17, 2014, https://www.rt.com/usa/retailers-hacker -attack-russian-750/.

4. Kevin Granville, "9 Recent Cyberattacks Against Big Businesses," *New York Times*, February 5, 2015, http://www.nytimes.com/interactive/2015/02/05 /technology/recent-cyberattacks.html.

5. Chris Isidore, "Target and Visa Reach $67 Million Deal in Hacking Case," CNN Money, August 18, 2015, http://money.cnn.com/2015/08/18/news /companies/target-visa-hack-deal/.

6. Elizabeth Weise, "IRS Hack Far Larger Than First Thought," *USA Today*, August 18, 2005, http://www.usatoday.com/story/tech/2015/08/17 /irs-hack-get-transcript/31864171/.

7. Robert W. Wood, "IRS Paid $5.8 Billion in Fraudulent Refunds, Identity Theft Efforts Need Work," *Forbes*, February 19, 2015, http://www.forbes.com /sites/robertwood/2015/02/19/irs-paid-5-8-billion-in-fraudulent-refunds -identity-theft-efforts-need-work/.

8. Government Accountability Office, GAO analysis of IRS data, GAO-15-119, January 2015, http://www.gao.gov/assets/670/667965.pdf.

9. Mark Hayward and Jason Schreiber, "Mayor Says No Wrongdoing with City Email Found on Cheating Site," *Union Leader*, August 24, 2015, http:// www.unionleader.com/article/20150825/NEWS0606/150829627/0/NEWS12.

10. Chris Isidore and David Goldman with contributors Erica Fink, Jose Pagliery, Charles Riley, and Laurie Segall, "Ashley Madison Hackers Post Millions of Customer Names," CNN Money, August 19, 2015, http://money .cnn.com/2015/08/18/technology/ashley-madison-data-dump/index.html.

11. Chris Isidore and David Goldman with contributors Erica Fink, Jose Pagliery, Charles Riley, and Laurie Segall, "Ashley Madison Hackers Post Millions of Customer Names," CNN Money, August 19, 2015, http://money.cnn.com/2015/08/18/technology/ashley-madison-data-dump/index.html

12. Sunny Freeman, "Ashley Madison Hack May Be Linked to Hate Crimes, Extortion, Suicide, Police Say," Toronto Star, August 24, 2015, http://www.thestar.com/business/2015/08/24/ashley-madison-hack-may-be-linked-to-suicides-police-say.html.

13. Sunny Freeman, "Ashley Madison Hack May Be Linked to Hate Crimes, Extortion, Suicide, Police Say," Toronto Star, August 24, 2015, http://www.thestar.com/business/2015/08/24/ashley-madison-hack-may-be-linked-to-suicides-police-say.html.

14. Eric Alt, "There's Now a $380,000 Bounty on the Heads of Ashley Madison Hackers," FastCompany, August 24, 2015, http://www.fastcompany.com/3050291/fast-feed/theres-now-a-380000-bounty-on-the-heads-of-ashley-madison-hackers.

15. Eric Alt, "There's Now a $380,000 Bounty on the Heads of Ashley Madison Hackers," FastCompany, August 24, 2015, http://www.fastcompany.com/3050291/fast-feed/theres-now-a-380000-bounty-on-the-heads-of-ashley-madison-hackers.

16. Yo Delmar, "Reviewing the U.S. Office of Personnel Management Data Breach," QualityDigest.com, August 19, 2015, http://www.qualitydigest.com/read/content_by_author/70780.

17. "US Official on China Hacking Government Database: 'This Is Deep'," Reuters, June 5, 2015, http://www.businessinsider.com/r-data-obtained-in-us-government-hack-dates-back-to-1985-us-official-2015-6.

18. Ellen Nakashima, "U.S. Decides Against Publicly Blaming China for Data Hack," Washington Post, July 21, 2015, https://www.washingtonpost.com/world/national-security/us-avoids-blaming-china-in-data-theft-seen-as-fair-game-in-espionage/2015/07/21/03779096-2eee-11e5-8353-1215475949f4_story.html.

19. "US Official on China Hacking Government Database: 'This Is Deep'," Reuters, June 5, 2015, http://www.businessinsider.com/r-data-obtained-in-us-government-hack-dates-back-to-1985-us-official-2015-6.

20. Lori Grisham, "Timeline: North Korea and the Sony Pictures Hack," USA Today Network, January 5, 2015, http://www.usatoday.com/story/news/nation-now/2014/12/18/sony-hack-timeline-interview-north-korea/20601645/.

21. Lori Grisham, "Timeline: North Korea and the Sony Pictures Hack," USA Today Network, January 5, 2015, http://www.usatoday.com/story/news/nation-now/2014/12/18/sony-hack-timeline-interview-north-korea/20601645/.

22. Lori Grisham, "Timeline: North Korea and the Sony Pictures Hack," *USA Today Network*, January 5, 2015, http://www.usatoday.com/story /news/nation-now/2014/12/18/sony-hack-timeline-interview-north-korea /20601645/.

CHAPTER 11: THE LEADERSHIP THAT BOARDS NEED NOW: THE MOST CRITICAL DYNAMICS ON TODAY'S BOARDS ARE HUMAN ONES

1. David Bogoslaw, "Appointing AI to Your Board," email newsletter correspondence from corporate secretary, July 25, 2011.

APPENDIX I: NAVIGATING THE MORASS OF CORPORATE JARGON: DON'T CHOKE ON ALPHABET SOUP (A GLOSSARY)

1. "Can You Tell What These Traders Are Talking About?," *Wall Street Journal*, September 14, 2015, originally published August 17, 2015, http:// graphics.wsj.com/quiz/?slug=glossary-of-bankers-trading-slang&standalone=1 &mod=e2tw.

2. "Can You Tell What These Traders Are Talking About?," *Wall Street Journal*, September 14, 2015, originally published August 17, 2015, http:// graphics.wsj.com/quiz/?slug=glossary-of-bankers-trading-slang&standalone=1 &mod=e2tw.

3. Public Company Accounting Oversight Board, Auditing Standard No. 14, Evaluating Audit Results, http://pcaobus.org/Standards/Auditing/Pages /Auditing_Standard_14_Appendix_B.aspx.

Index

About the Authors

JOHN T. MONTFORD is president and chief executive officer of JTM Consulting, LLC, a state and federal government relations advisory firm he founded in 2010. Montford has had many diverse and varied careers in law, business, politics, education, and philanthropy. He is a graduate of the University of Texas in Austin where he received both bachelor and Jurist Doctor degrees. Following law school he served on active duty as an officer in the United States Marine Corps. After his military service he returned to Texas to practice law. He served as an elected District attorney and was subsequently elected to the Texas Senate where he served for 14 years. During his tenure in the Senate, he served as Chair of the Senate State Affairs and Senate Finance Committees. Texas Monthly named Senator Montford as one of the "Top Ten Best Legislates" for five sessions. In 1996 Montford left the Senate upon being appointed as the first Chancellor of the Texas Tech University System, the system's Chief Executive Officer. In 2001 Montford was named Chancellor Emeritus. That year he left academia to become President, External Affairs for Southwestern Bell Telephone Company and Southern New England Telephone Company. He also held several executive positions in the telecommunications industry including Senior Vice President for State Legislative affairs for SBC and President of the Western Region for AT&T Services. From 2010 until 2012 Montford was Senior Advisor and Consultant for Global Public Policy for General Motors Company. He also served as Chair of the GM Foundation Board and was a member of the GM Executive Committee. During his many careers he has served as a director on several for-profit, not-for-profit, and charitable boards. Since 2002 he has served as an Independent Director on the Southwest Airlines Board. Currently he serves as Chair of the Audit Committee. Other positions he has held include Chair of the San Antonio Chamber of Commerce, Chair of the San Antonio Economic Development Foundation, President and Chair of the National Western Art Foundation's Briscoe Museum, Chair of the Advisory Committee for Texas Parks and Wildlife Department and Chair of the Development Board for the University of Texas Health Science Center at San Antonio. Montford's works have been published in several law review articles and he co-authored a book on Texas Worker's Compensation.

JOSEPH DANIEL McCOOL is principal of The McCool Group, a global advisory firm that helps companies, universities, and not-for-profit organizations get better results from executive search, management succession, and the board nominating process. For nearly 20 years, McCool has been a source for business insights as well as expert commentary on board and executive search and succession issues in global media, including *The Wall Street Journal*, *The Financial Times*, *The Chronicle of Higher Education*, and *The Economist*. McCool has also appeared on BBC World News, CNBC, CBC Radio, and CNN Radio, among other global media. He is the author of *Deciding Who Leads: How Executive Recruiters Drive, Direct & Disrupt the Global Search for Leadership Talent* and serves on corporate and institutional advisory boards. He holds a master's degree in organizational leadership with a certificate in servant leadership from Gonzaga University and a bachelor's degree in business administration from Plymouth State College of the University System of New Hampshire. McCool has been a member of the National Association of Corporate Directors (NACD), the Society of Corporate Secretaries & Governance Professionals, the Human Resources Leadership Forum, and the National Eagle Scout Association.